hey you!

A CAREER

ON A

CAN TURN
BIG IDEA

hey you!

pitch to win in an ideas economy

Will Murray

www.yourmomentum.com
the stuff that drives you

What is momentum?

Momentum is a completely new publishing philosophy, in print and online, dedicated to giving you more of the information, inspiration and drive to enhance who you are, what you do, and how you do it.

Fusing the changing forces of work, life and technology, momentum will give you the right stuff for a brighter future and set you on the way to being all you can be.

Who needs momentum?

Momentum is for people who want to make things happen in their careers and their lives, who want to work at something they enjoy and that's worthy of their talents and their time.

Momentum people have values and principles, and question who they are, what they do, and who for. Wherever they work, they want to feel proud of what they do. And they are hungry for information, stimulation, ideas and answers …

Momentum online

Visit *www.yourmomentum.com* to be part of the talent community. Here you'll find a full listing of current and future books, an archive of articles by momentum authors, sample chapters and self-assessment tools. While you're there, post your work/life questions to our momentum coaches and sign up to receive free newsletters with even more stuff to drive you.

More momentum

If you need more drive for your life, try one of these titles, all published under the momentum label:

good idea:

explosive thinking

changes the world

great idea:

ideapreneurs
have mastered
explosive thinking

brilliant idea:

anyone can become an ideapreneur

PEARSON EDUCATION LIMITED

Head Office
Edinburgh Gate
Harlow CM20 2JE
Tel: +44 (0)1279 623623
Fax: +44 (0)1279 431059

London Office:
128 Long Acre, London WC2E 9AN
Tel: +44 (0)20 7447 2000
Fax: +44 (0)20 7240 5771
Website: www.business-minds.com

First published in Great Britain in 2001

© Pearson Education Limited 2001

The right of Will Murray to be identified as
author of this work has been asserted by him
in accordance with the Copyright, Designs and
Patents Act 1988.

ISBN 1843 04009 3

British Library Cataloguing in Publication Data
A CIP catalogue record for this book can be
obtained from the British Library.

10 9 8 7 6 5 4 3 2 1

Typeset by Northern Phototypesetting Co. Ltd,
Bolton
Printed and bound in Great Britain by
Biddles Ltd, Guildford and King's Lynn

Cover design by Heat
Text design by Claire Brodmann Book Designs,
Lichfield, Staffs.

The Publishers' policy is to use paper
manufactured from sustainable forests.

dedication...

to george and henry:

always live in hope,
strive to change the world,
travel with those you love,

be extraordinary not ordinary.

thank you....

to Sarah Sweet Rowley and Annalese Banbury, thanks for all of your explosive suggestions, TLC, and the late nights we put in to add the finishing touches

to David Turner, David has been fantastic (as always) – thanks for all of your time and support

to Rachael Stock at Pearson Education who has been great – thanks for your energy, Rachael, and for laughing at the right bits!

to Sarah Heathcote who has been a brilliant researcher – thanks for all of your help, Sarah

to Sean Blair for his foreword and to all of the contributors, Matt Marsh, Richard James, Mike Mathieson, David Stuart, John Cross, Richard Seymour, Stuart Armstrong and Mike Weber, thanks for sharing the secrets of true Ideapreneurs

Thank you, Mum, Dad, George and Henry, for being yourselves

opening

section one
ideation radiation

section two
imagineering explosive ideas

section three
constructing incendiary campaigns

section four
exploding on the scene

opening

hey you

momentum

closing

foreword

Will's been on the coke again – only this time it's *not* decaffeinated! In this highly charged book you will be challenged and cajoled, bullied and berated, inspired and bull whipped out of your nice comfort bubble into what I will now think of as … 'Will's World'.

It's an explosive place – not for the frail, weak-hearted or for those with a bad hangover. Do not attempt to enact the contents of this book while operating heavy machinery or while driving.

You may not agree with all you see in Will's world, you may feel uncomfortable in Will's world … and that's the point. Welcome to the future!

Explosive Thinking is kind of like lateral thinking on a steroids / Prozac combo. Think fire not water, think boom not pop, think laser not light bulb.

Ideapreneurs in Will's world are Time Lords, Masters of the Dark Side, Knights of the Round Table. Think zealots with big shiny idea sticks. They are the people who surf the very edge of the froth of chaos, and don't get wet – they don't even need wax on their board. In fact board, what board?

Critically, *Hey You!* is a new kind of book for a new kind of millennium. It's a cross between Kurt Vonnegut and Delia Smith – a kind of how to bake a 'Dominate the Universe pie'. When I own my own copy I'll tear the spine off, plastic-encapsulate the pages and randomly paper the walls of my shower with it. *Wow*, what a way to start the day – a kind of loofa for the seratonin gland in my brain. I'd be taking my first step towards being an Ideapreneur. Today the shower, tomorrow the world!!!! grRRraaAAGGGHHHHHH!!!!

Uncoil the wire, light the fuse, stand well back. Be afraid, very afraid – Ideapreneurs are coming to a town near you and they're exploding with ideas that will change the world!

Sean Blair

Limited Nowhere

welcome

You only have to look back a couple of hundred years to see how a small number of truly explosive ideas have changed our lives forever. Electricity, the telephone, TV, personal computers and the internet are just a few of the most obvious examples.

And it's not just inventions – over many years people like Leonardo Da Vinci, Galileo and Darwin have totally changed the way we think about the world and even our understanding of ourselves. Vincent Van Gogh, Picasso and friends had such radical ideas that they turned the accepted view of art totally on its head.

So how did all these people do it? Well it wasn't easy – we all know the lengths Van Gogh was driven to, for example.

In the real world people resist change to the status quo at every turn. If you wanted to achieve what these stars of the past achieved, you needed guts, determination, a lifetime of dedication and sometimes even a willingness to lay down your life in a blaze of firewood and glory. Now that's what I call commitment!

And have you noticed *this* mega change? People aren't making money out of farming, or fishing, or manufacturing any more. They don't even have time to make big money out of feeding or serving people. Today's top talent creates an idea, generates buy-in, gets the ball rolling, sells out for a fortune and moves on. Today's Rockefellers and Rothschilds are all in the ideas business.

To quote Nathan Myhrvold, former Chief Technology Officer at Microsoft:

'Workers with good ideas, or the ability to generate good ideas, can write their own ticket.

A great employee is worth a thousand times an average one because of the quality of their ideas.'

Today you need to be busy, busy, busy changing the world. You need new tools to help you get places faster – it's now totally a first-come, first-served world.

you need great ideas!

you need to spread you ideas fast

you need explosive thinking

you need to become

an ideapreneur!

What makes ideapreneurs really special?

Ideapreneurs are Masters of Explosive Thinking.

These are the people who always seem to get it right. They set up internet companies when most people still thought that a mouse was something furry. They set up restaurants when nouvelle cuisine was still nouvelle. These people know rising stars before they have even risen over the horizon and they go to future cult films before they've premiered. And you thought these people were just born lucky? No, they're Explosive Thinkers.

And what exactly is explosive thinking?

explosive thinking

multiplies your power and purpose

explosive thinking

multiplies your ideas

explosive thinking

multiplies the power and purpose of your ideas

It's not the wham-bam thank you ma'am, going in with all guns blazing that it sounds. Explosive Thinking is actually a way of life. It is controlled, dedicated and passionate belief in idea generation and most importantly, it produces explosive results.

Explosive Thinking isn't just about taking explosive action, it's about explosive results.

And how do you learn to become an Ideapreneur and master Explosive Thinking?

Mind play

The answer to that is training.

To help you become an Ideapreneur rather than just read about their virtues, we have created Mind Play, an explosive new fitness programme for the brain with 52 weekly workouts.

Mind Play is designed to exercise your mind, allowing you to radically expand your existing thought processes.

To make room for Explosive Thinking there is one vital thing to remember. Jettison any old ideas and mind sets that you will no longer need, because as an Ideapreneur, you can't afford to have a cluttered mind.

Your brain isn't getting any bigger, and if you are like me, it might even be getting a bit worn about the edges, but like the most truly remarkable women's handbags, it is still amazing what you can pull out of it.

Hey You! will help you learn to unlearn.

01

section one
ideation radiation

hey you

moment um

IDEAS

... TODAY,

NO LONGER BELONG BELONG TO BUSINESS...

BUSINESS BELONGS TO IDEAS.

hey you

momentum

chapter one
our exploding world

'Seeing your moment is one thing, seizing it is everything.'

David Turner

If you read the *Financial Times* tomorrow, you will come across as many ideas in one day as the average 17th-century person confronted in a whole lifetime.

What does this mean to you?

Knowledge is now passé. Everyone has access to so much knowledge that they can always find a great reason for not doing almost anything.

It is time to stop thinking about knowledge. Instead breathe it as you would air, sip it like water, dine on it like a Big Mac and fries, but never let it define your universe and dominate your hopes and dreams.

The Knowledge Economy is officially dead – welcome to the Human Economy.

The human economy switches power from companies to the people, in the shape of employees, partners and customers. In the same way that the industrial revolution led to the consumer economy as a result of mass production, the internet has generated the human economy as the result of the power it has given the individual.

Player power

In football today, the explosion of player power and the likely destruction of the transfer system is transferring value from clubs to key players.

The same is happening to the rest of us. Whatever field you work in, movers and shakers are becoming less reliant on and more independent from the 'corporate shells' they work for. The future for all of us is to shift inexorably forward from single careers towards multi-projects and contract browsing.

So why is the world turning on its head?

Why is corporate conformity becoming personal mobility?

Why has the worm turned?

Speed wins

Sometimes I sing a lullaby to George and Henry when I'm trying to get them to sleep. Partly because of my singing voice and partly because I have one clear objective, I keep the lyrics simple:

'Sleepy, sleepy, sleepy, sleepy, sleepy, sleepy, sleepy, sleep.'

It's simple, memorable and it works.

The reason I'm telling this rather bizarre little tale is that the exploding world requires the same sort of mental focus, except instead of 'sleepy, sleepy' it's:

'Speedy, speedy, speedy, speedy, speedy, speedy, speedy, speed.'

There isn't much else to say. If you're not fast you're last, or at best you're a support act, but more than likely you'll end up sitting in the audience.

The 60/90 rule

In the old days, when you had a good idea you milked it for as long as you could until you had it at least 90 per cent perfect or you had extracted 90 per cent of the value. Not any more – in the exploding world, by the time you are 60 per cent through your idea, you'll be out of time. Let it go and move on – ideas are becoming victims of diminishing returns.

Your value to time ratio will nosedive as others get in on your act. Fortune now favours the fickle.

Look at it like this, if you own a thoroughbred champion racehorse you could use it to pull your cart, but you don't – you buy an old cart-horse to pull the cart and keep the racehorse purely for racing where it can earn you big money.

The same applies to winners now – they don't keep turning over an old idea just because they can. They would rather use their most precious resource, which is their time, creating and exploding new ideas where they get the best return.

Transparency

There's nowhere to hide today – transparency is one of the most significant aspects of our exploding world. Both people and companies are going to face the same sort of scrutiny experienced by celebrities. Make sure your pitch adds up and don't rest on your laurels, or you may find someone has mown your lawn!

With the growing intrusion of the internet and the mushrooming of narrow-interest websites, those that want to can now see round the back of company facades. Companies are starting to resemble open-plan offices – people get to see what you are up to as well as what you produce and how you promote yourself.

Ideas as the new competition

You can't forget return on investment, market share, profitability or any of the usual business ratios and controls any more now than you ever could. The dot com disasters who thought the laws of business had magically been suspended are living examples of this fact.

But at the other end of the spectrum, the basis of competition has flipped over diametrically from things to ideas. It's not about being a monopoly in a mature market or the most established company in the drugs industry any more. Today, it's about being the newest, the most wanted, and the most talked about. You need to be the hippest new website or the coldest brand. (For those not in the know, cool has become so cool that the very coolest things are now cold, not hot as they used to be. Clear? If not, ask your kids.)

The things companies used to rely on for differentiation are now dodo food.

Price, advertising, technology and products have been reduced to a level playing field by the instant nature of our economy, transparency, connectivity and the global reach of the internet.

It is a sobering thought that, within five years, half of today's companies may not have survived and will have been replaced by younger, fitter, more flexible companies that either haven't yet been formed or are still trading out of someone's bedroom. Sit back and watch many of today's biggest names crash and burn.

And if this is true for companies then, boy, as an individual you are in for some major changes too.

Individuals don't have the same options as companies. For people, going bust is 100 per cent terminal and instead of shareholders, you have partners and kids who need you.

hey you

Migrating value

In the human economy, 90 per cent of value will be added, either at the very start or at the very end of the production process. At one end, there's the launch and creation of new ideas and at the other, delivery of extreme customer experience. The people stuck in the middle have got plenty to worry about.

Counting the cost

Relying on broadcasting outbound messages via traditional advertising media is becoming a doom-laden experience.

Advertising is tediously slow to produce, exorbitantly expensive and most of it goes in one eye and out the other.

Add to this the fragmentation of channels to your target market, especially with digital TV and web-based media, and the scale of the new communication dilemma becomes clear.

Making the most of the alternatives to mass outbound communication is key – where advertising might still be good for creating mass impact it won't cut it with relationship building. Gone are the days when advertising was the only answer. Today you need to combine it with clever personal networking and some creative alternative thinking to create incendiary campaigns.

To make matters worse, people are becoming immune to the overkill of glossy advert images and messages they face at every turn. Instead people are becoming more likely to respond to a recommendation from a friend on a quick e-mail.

Transfer this pattern to people level and you have the same issue. The standard PowerPoint presentation can still act as the rubber stamp to your proposal, but it's becoming wiser to keep the obvious stuff to last. You still need to hold the meeting, but it's time to make it more explosive. Start getting to those you need when they don't expect it, have something to offer *before* not *after* you need help, be likeable, act with sophistication, appeal to emotions and put yourself about a bit.

Generation e-mail

Kids today view e-mail and text messaging the way we used to view street corners. It's fast, it's quirky and you can make it your oyster.

Think flash mail, not direct mail, and your idea's with your audience in minutes.

If you want to do it and you can, learn like lightning, chill out, schmooze in a chat room and make e-mail your new best friend.

Did you read about that poor girl who sent her boyfriend a saucy e-mail extolling the virtues of her sexual technique? With the benefit of easily addressed e-mails, it had been forwarded to literally tens of millions of people within days. It closed down a couple of corporate mainframes, with the pure volume of 'traffic' and resulted in a media scrum outside her house within less than a week.

Such is the power of e-mail finger.

E-mail and the web are not about doing old stuff better:

The web is now the gunpowder of ideas.

So much noise

Great news then, we have this fabulous new world driving our ideas with brave new thinking. The bad news is that you won't be the only one to realize this. Our exploding world is becoming noisier than 50,000 teenage girls screaming at a Westlife concert.

In today's market the people making it big are those who get heard above the din. These guys jump out of the crowd on to the stage, they're the stars who combine great ideas with stardust and even make money before their bubble bursts.

Big is beautiful.

Sorry guys, but size matters.

hey you

momentum

The great news, though, is that big today means big heart and big impact, not big cheese, or big organization, where size hinders more than helps.

We can't all be heavyweights, but we can all punch above our weight. Going in hard, fast and furious every now and then has far more impact than continuous non-stop effort. Future success will be for those who choose to invest their time, effort and money wisely and act with the courage of their convictions. In the exploding world, the things that work cost time and effort, not money, and this is the clever bit.

Big hitters are realizing that the only way to learn is to try things out fast, review progress non-stop and, if it comes to it, learn what you can and quickly cut your losses. Think again and start over before the others are even out of the starting blocks for the first time.

So how do you do this? Try becoming an Ideapreneur.

OUR EXPLODING WORLD

- ◆ Seizing your moment is everything.
- ◆ Corporate conformity is becoming personal mobility.
- ◆ Fortune favours the fickle.
- ◆ Constantly developing new ideas brings the highest returns.
- ◆ Think flash mail, not direct mail.
- ◆ Kids today view e-mail the way we viewed street corners.
- ◆ The web is the gunpowder of ideas.

TRIGGER

Try it, learn fast, cut your losses and start again before others even wake up.

chapter two
the extraordinary world of the ideapreneur

If the world is exploding, who's going to thrive on the newly released energy and who's going to suffer the fallout?

The new masters of the universe are going to be Ideapreneurs, free from the burden of traditional overheads and using ideas like light sabres.

So what makes Ideapreneurs tick?

The magic ingredients of Ideapreneurs are:

◆ speed

◆ strength

◆ insight

◆ determination.

Using these four ingredients, Ideapreneurs drive both the way they draw inspiration and the way they capitalize on their ideas. They unite speed and strength to generate power, the same way as mass and velocity deliver momentum, and they combust their insight and determination to multiply their purpose.

Power and purpose are the hallmarks of the Ideapreneur.

What does each ingredient contribute to an Ideapreneur?

Speed

◆ Radio took 20 years to gain 10 million users.

◆ TV took ten years to gain 10 million users.

◆ Netscape took two years to gain 10 million users.

◆ Hotmail took half a year to gain 10 million users.

Speed is clearly a significant issue!

So what are Ideapreneurs doing to make them fast?

Explosive speed

Ideapreneurs:

◆ act first and ask questions later

◆ are naturally better connected

◆ use detonators to explode their ideas

◆ oil their ideas to make them slippery

◆ stretch their ideas to fit the world

◆ use design as a natural act to create immediate impact

◆ have mastered the art of creative charging to rip down any barriers to entry.

Strength

Which elements of Explosive Thinking combine to make Ideapreneurs strong?

Explosive strength

Ideapreneurs:

- know that if they can't be Number One, not to bother

- paint powerful pictures to get their idea adopted

- destroy markets' core beliefs and watch them implode

- thrive on anarchy to disable their opponents

- dominate their markets from the inside out

- know that if it's not amazing not to go there

- live and die personal relationships.

Insight

Why are Ideapreneurs insightful?

Explosive Insight

Ideapreneurs:

- understand that peer pressure succeeds where advertising fears to tread

- embark on crusades rather than starting wars

- draw their strength from everything that surrounds them.

Insight-driven inspiration

Insight dominates the way Ideapreneurs draw their inspiration.

You can't achieve a complete paradigm shift in thinking or break through a taboo using one-way thinking – it just won't cut it. You need more, much more. You need to use four elements, anarchy, karma, magic and nurture, to achieve what one-way thinking can't. This is the essence of insight.

Fusing together anarchy, karma, magic and nurture into an explosive mix, Ideapreneurs use insight to create ideas that move faster than shoppers on the first day of Harrods' sale.

And the miracle of insight comes not from any individual element of the mix but from the Ideapreneur's ability to draw from each separate element at will.

Let's look at each one.

Anarchy

Anarchy is your killer instinct, your tough side, the Mr Angry that breaks out and scares people from time to time. It ensures that when the going gets tough, you get going. **Anarchy makes you invincible.**

Anarchy is your black/scarlet side.

Karma

Maybe this should be calmer. Karma is your voice of reason, the lake of tranquillity from which your inspiration flows. Without karma you are a storm that will ultimately blow out. **Karma lets you see what others are too blind to see.**

Karma is your cream/limpid-blue side.

Magic

Magic is your Merlin factor, the part of you that creates stardust out of sawdust. Magic is your elixir, it makes you special, charismatic and unforgettable. **Magic turns you into a star.**

Magic is your purple/gold side.

Nurture

No man is an island, so nurture connects you to people, it helps you understand, empathize with and care for those around you. **Nurture inspires others to follow you.**

Nurture is your green/rich-orange side.

The mark of the Master Ideapreneur is their unerring ability to retreat into, and be refreshed from, each element of their explosive mix.

Determination

The last of the four ingredients, determination, combines with insight to fashion the Ideapreneur's renowned purpose. Determination is the backbone of the spirit in which Ideapreneurs live their lives.

It's the combination of several elements of Explosive Thinking that make Ideapreneurs determined.

Explosive Determination

Ideapreneurs:

◆ hold their own cards and master their own destiny

◆ focus on what's real and never give it up

◆ allow others to make mistakes for them.

Determination to Succeed

Determination shapes the lives and learning of Ideapreneurs. Ideapreneurs never stop training and they never stop developing, 52 weeks a year.

THE EXTRAORDINARY WORLD OF THE IDEAPRENEUR

◆ Power and purpose are the hallmarks of the Ideapreneur.

◆ Speed drives Ideapreneurs, strength empowers their thinking.

◆ Insight determines the way Ideapreneurs draw inspiration.

◆ Anarchy makes Ideapreneurs invincible.

◆ Karma lets them see what others are too blind to see.

◆ Magic turns Ideapreneurs into stars and nurture inspires others to follow them.

◆ Determination is their backbone.

TRIGGER

Free from the burden of traditional overheads, Ideapreneurs use ideas like light sabres.

hey you

chapter three
explosive thinking

If the world's exploding and you want to become an Ideapreneur, what should you be doing?

You need to keep pace with the market, you need explosive results, you need Explosive Thinking.

What then is Explosive Thinking, apart from a snappy title, I hear you ask?

Explosive Thinking goes where viral ideas fear to tread.

Viral thinking is already revolutionizing the spreading of ideas. No more big-bang, knock-their-heads-together advertising. With viral thinking you create your idea and as the name implies, you spread it the same way a virus spreads. E-mailing is the lifeblood of viral thinking; once an idea is sneezed out it spreads through the ether as fast as its infectiousness will carry it.

You don't have to be a genius to work out that the idea virus is a fantastic breakthrough on both the personal and corporate level, but is it the complete story? Does every silver lining have a cloud? Unfortunately, yes.

Viral ideas spread faster than flu in February but just like the flu, viral thinking can be a right pain.

◆ Once it's out there you lose control over it.

◆ People are quick to build up resistance.

◆ The elderly and infirm are most likely to fall for it (metaphorically speaking).

◆ Viruses mutate fast.

◆ Viruses live for themselves, not for you.

You can never own a virus.

This is where Explosive Thinking comes in.

Although you may not know it yet, Explosive Thinking:

◆ puts you in control

◆ is irresistible

◆ gets you there time and again

◆ has power and purpose

◆ creates explosive results.

Explosive Thinking always delivers value to *you* the thinker.

Explosive Thinking is a way of life, not an occasional act. Explosive Thinkers are often part of a team riding on the crest of a wave, creating idea value, not product value. While busily sweeping up the cash and banking it, they are already planning how to start the next wave.

Use new ideas, not acquired knowledge; think things, don't do things.

hey you

Explosive facts

1. Early birds

Time and Explosive Thinkers wait for no man. Gone are the days when you had to get all your ducks in a row before you ventured into the marketplace. Explosive Thinkers seed their ideas at the first opportunity they get.

You won't go big bang if the market isn't already desperate for you. How do Explosive Thinkers make an early move? Any which way they can, formal, informal, fair, unfair, and they don't hide their light under a bushel.

THE MORAL   **Act first, ask questions later**

2. Get together

Personal networking is becoming the new Stock Exchange.

Networking may be as old as the hills but it still works. It doesn't matter whether it's personal networking we're talking about or Tupperware, if you are not networking you are missing out.

All the most successful people and companies in the world are networkers, which is part of why they get places others can't.

THE MORAL   **Be naturally better connected**

3. Detonation

We know networking is good but there's more to it than getting your idea credo front of mind with every person you can think of. Explosive Thinkers target the critical few. Some people in your chosen audience will not only be proven communicators, they will have immense influence with the rest of your target audience.

Win a 'detonator's' heart and they'll explode your idea better than you ever can.

These are the people you need on your side. They may be celebs, senior managers or influential people in general; they're the ones your target audience will believe.

THE MORAL Use detonators to explode your idea

4. Nice and easy does it

Why do some people make it so tough for the very people they want to embrace and evangelize their ideas? The number of websites that are difficult to navigate is still staggering, with ambition often overriding common sense.

Even worse for Explosive Thinkers is how hard it can be to print out interesting bits in an easy format or, God forbid, to forward these bits to a friend.

Explosive Thinkers make it easy for detonators to do their job. Right from the first spark they make their idea simple to communicate, both for them and others involved in their explosion.

I read a book once called *Silicon Snake Oil*. Explosive Thinkers rub this in every day.

Elements of your idea will need to stay secret, but for the most part the wider and faster things spread the better – make sure these bits are well oiled. First get your idea culture right, then look at your website, your intranet, which media you use and how easy it is for key contacts to spread your idea.

THE MORAL Oil your idea

5. Lift and stretch

Explosive ideas are no respecters of international borders. *You* may be quite happy exploiting a cosy local market but Explosive Ideas aren't. All the best tools for transmitting ideas travel the world faster than hot gossip, Explosive Thinkers plan ahead to exploit this.

Whether it's the whole world or your world that you are aiming to change, you need partners. Working in a big company these can be divisions in other countries; for entrepreneurs these can be friends and relatives based overseas. Whatever your idea, if it works in one country it will work in many. Sell the idea for others to put into practice, never ever leave ideas fallow.

THE MORAL   **Stretch your idea to fit the world**

6. Designed to work

Design is never an afterthought to Explosive Thinkers.

Design has become a way of life for people who maximize every chance life gives them. Close your eyes and think of the *Life* magazine cover, Superman, the Penguin Books trademark, a Monopoly box, an Oscar, a Chanel perfume bottle, Mickey Mouse, Elvis Presley, or even the man confronting tanks in Beijing. I don't know about you, but when I close my eyes I can see these things as though they are there in front of me. This is the power of design that Explosive Thinkers understand implicitly.

The difference in explosive power between a beautifully designed idea and an ill-designed one is phenomenal. Every element of your idea can benefit from design. Brand your proposal, brand your product, any packaging can be either an object of desire or functional chic. Any physical product can be the personification of your credo and any physical experience can be your credo in action. Explosive Thinkers won't even get into bed unless it's well designed.

THE MORAL   **Without design you are just a thing**

7. Charge!

This is an absolute cornerstone of Explosive Thinking. Managing the migration from free to finance is the key skill of an Explosive Thinker and one of the main differentiators between an Explosive Idea and an idea virus.

You may need the resources of others to enhance your idea. But maintain the upper hand. Get the balance between having all of the resources you need and ensuring there's still plenty in it for you.

The same issue applies at a market level – you have to overcome the contradiction between low cost of entry, or even free entry, and the need to earn big money within a short payback time.

What's the answer?

Sell your credo, not just your audience benefit, and never be too shy to ask for your money. Think laterally about the art of how you charge – this is one of the best areas to destroy the market's core beliefs. Look at how others make money and attack its weakest points. Think the unthinkable because it may well work. When it comes to money you can never be too lateral.

Get your tariff right and you'll move faster than a Ford Cortina with go-faster stripes and fluffy dice.

THE MORAL   **Master-charging rips down any barriers to entry**

8. Life's not fair

Do you want to be in the Premiership or the League? Explosive Thinking recognizes that rewards don't come equally. First prize 100 points, second prize 20 points, third five points and beyond that you are doing it for love. This isn't new in itself but two things are:

◆ The gap between pole position and the rest is dramatically widening.

◆ Explosive Thinkers move in fast, then move on to new markets where they can earn the mega bucks again.

With rate of return on both effort and investment going up and down faster than a tart's skirt, why milk an idea for every last penny when dominating new ideas brings the high returns?

9. Create your idea credo

Credos go beyond sound bites and manifestos.

Your credo is the living, breathing, spirit of your idea, encapsulated with clarity and passion. Never pass 'Go' until your credo is totally clear or your explosion ends up resembling nothing but a brief rumble (not unlike trapped wind) or the Tower of Babel on a bad day.

Explosive Thinkers take the time to illuminate their credo in a way that creates immediate and empathic impact because they know their idea depends on it.

10. Destroy their core beliefs

Sun Tzu said that if you defeat your enemy's strategy, you defeat your enemy. We say that if you can destroy your market's core beliefs you can mould the world to your own design. Strike at their core beliefs and watch their empire collapse like a house of cards.

At the heart of Explosive Thinking is killer insight. Look deeper than others, challenge hard at the things your opponents hold most dear. Be relentless in your thinking – Explosive Thinkers take no prisoners.

The most obvious recent example of this is the vacuum market, which was built on the idea that vacuum cleaners need bags to capture dust and was keeping alive a very healthy bag supply business. James Dyson carved up the market by destroying the premise that vacuum cleaners must have bags. The rest is history.

11. Anarchy rules

Explosive ideas thrive on anarchy. They gorge on uncertainty like crocodiles on stampeding wildebeest. If a market is in turmoil, either because you have imploded it with a killer insight or because it is just new, impetuous and innocent, then explode all over it. Swamp opinion formers by blitzing the market, contradict the latest ideas and be controversial, send out misleading distractions, then hit hard and fast where your opponents least expect it. Every Explosive Thinker has a warm cuddly side but now is the time to be ruthless.

THE MORAL Thriving on anarchy disables your opponents

12. Domination (if that's OK)

Better to own 100 per cent of ten than ten per cent of 100. Aim for the biggest market for your idea that you can, but never bite off more than you can chew. If you need to convince a group to act, don't settle for a majority view – keep striving for 100 per cent agreement behind your idea. Any less and the door will always be open to subversive behaviour.

Domination is to Explosive Thinkers what a pond is to a frog, home sweet home.

When you invade a market, don't think you can invade half of it. Take over half a market and be forever watching your back; conquer the whole market like the Romans did Britain and be remembered for thousands of years.

How do Explosive Thinkers dominate a marketplace? They start by totally dominating the minds of just a small percentage of their market or key audience. Turn five per cent of your audience into idea zealots and, as discussed, they will detonate the rest.

13. Amaze your friends

I don't know whether you are a fan of magic shows but some magicians are utterly amazing, just as Houdini was. They perform tricks that defy belief by working in a separate sphere of consciousness to their audience, combined with extreme fitness and total agility. The flip side is that audience expectation rises by the day and some of what was amazing 20 years ago is cringe-worthy now.

So with ideas – Explosive Thinkers pull rabbits out of hats before breakfast and cut people in half for lunch. Amazing behaviour is the only acceptable behaviour and it isn't as hard as it may seem.

Companies talk about customer satisfaction, they review satisfaction, and they have satisfaction performance measures, and lo and behold that is the best they ever achieve. If they measured customer delight, performed to delight, and learnt what delights individual customers, they would actually start delighting their customers and they might even generate customer love. Explosive Thinkers work the same way – everything they think about is subject to these questions: 'Is this delightful, extraordinary and amazing?'

14. Lock them up

This builds on the previous point. Once they've got a buyer for their idea either as a detonator or end user, Explosive Thinkers hang on to them and don't let go until they are ready to sell and move on. Build up the interaction with both customers and contacts – the more you converse, the more you learn about each other and the stronger the bond gets between you. No junk mail, though, or dreadful outbound telemarketing – make everything personal.

15. Get out of my face

Talk with me, not at me. Years ago when commercial TV and the like were launched, people were so grateful for some entertainment and choice that they would put up with almost anything. Now times have changed and choice is a given, but the core principles of most advertising are stuck in a groove.

Why do people still think the best way to talk to someone is to stop them doing what they are enjoying and shout at them? Get real! This isn't just a rant against advertising – it will always have a role to play in both image creation and info transfer – but it's not the only answer. If you do need to use it, make it part of an overall Explosive Campaign.

The same applies to selling a personal idea – stop relying on formal channels, use your head, learn about your audience, become an unintrusive part of their life and create your own Explosive Campaign.

Explosive Campaigns kick in only when the people you want to sell your idea to are the ones selling your idea to each other. Who do *you* trust? A friend, a colleague, or an impersonal presentation or advert?

Create interest and involvement instead of booking space.

THE MORAL **Peer pressure succeeds where advertising fears to tread**

16. Crusaders

Explosive Thinkers are not into doing things by half. When they want to change the world they embark on a crusade. They identify worthy causes linked to their idea and mobilize people behind them. Firing up cause-related passion definitely works, but don't try just being clever about it. Any link must be genuine and an Explosive

Thinker must be prepared to support their crusade personally. One of the people I work with, Caroline Turner, is about to take part in a 26-mile power walk where all participants walk baring their bras to earn money in support of breast cancer. Guess who is sponsoring the event? Wonderbra.

THE MORAL Embark on a crusade, don't start a war

17. Inner belief

If you want to be an Explosive Thinker you can't be one-dimensional. Explosive Thinkers draw inspiration and strength from all aspects of their psyche.

Inner calm and communing with those around you are as essential to success as stardust and strength.

THE MORAL Draw your strength from everything that surrounds you

18. Channel masters

With personal insecurity becoming more global than Coca-Cola, only those mastering their own destiny will be able to sleep easy.

Channel masters are at the top of their own food chains. They decide when they want to work, who they want to work with, what on and why. Channel masters have an extensive web of contacts, all of whom are important but none of whom are crucial to their survival. They work for people, with people and have others working for them. They are resilient, proactive and have every reason to be confident.

You don't have to be Bill Gates.

You don't have to be in big business.

You do need to know what's best for you.

THE MORAL Hold your own cards and master your own destiny

19. Never say die

Explosive Thinkers never give up. Being more than prepared to lose a battle, they'll fight you on the beaches before they lose the war. They know what game they're in – ideas are their current vehicle, not their life. Explosive Thinkers know they can always mutate ideas or develop new ideas fast. Like the SAS they believe 'he who dares wins'. Audacious both in attack and strategic withdrawal, Explosive Thinkers live to see another day, but like Arnold Schwarzenegger, 'they'll be back'.

THE MORAL Focus on what's real and never give it up

20. The harder I work the luckier I get

It is no accident that Explosive Thinkers think and behave the way they do. It's not natural talent, it's hard work, dedication and training. Most Explosive Thinkers have identified and studied a master to model their thinking on. It may be someone they know or someone well known. Even if they don't actually know their mentor to start with, the most adroit Explosive Thinkers will make sure that they get to know them eventually, one way or another.

If you want to be an Explosive Thinker, you don't have time to make all your own mistakes – let others make them for you and learn their lessons the easy way. *Everyone* needs a mentor; whether president of the United States, a CEO or a house person, don't be too proud to find a real-life mentor who has the experience to help you make the important decisions. And you can always read a good book.

THE MORAL Allow others to make mistakes for you

EXPLOSIVE THINKING

- Destroy a market's core beliefs.

- Make your idea so real that others can cuddle it.

- Let others detonate your ideas for you.

- Dominate your chosen zones from the inside out.

- Relax your audience.

- Master the art of asking for money.

- Travel the whole world and make it yours.

Trigger:

Explosive Thinking creates explosive results, blowing opponents out of the water.

TRIGGER

Explosive Thinking creates explosive results, blowing opponents out of the water.

chapter four
ideapreneurs at large

'The desire for knowledge, like the thirst for riches, increases ever with the acquisition of it.'

Laurence Sterne

'Knowledge is the only instrument of production that is not subject to diminishing returns.'

John Maurice Clark

But ultimately:

Knowledge is merely sand on a beach until an Ideapreneur transforms it, oyster-like, into a pearl.

We know that Ideapreneurs are bound together by a creative purpose, a constructive power and a passion for pitching, but what are they like as people?

Richard Branson and Bill Gates might be considered as obvious examples, but on this occasion far too obvious, so we'll choose to ignore them this time.

To gain a flavour of how real-life Ideapreneurs work, I spoke to some who are out there every day and asked them about the source of their motivations, vision and creativity.

Enter the minds of masters

Q. In terms of your creativity, where does your passion fit in?

A. 'Passion always flavours my creativity. I will only work on a project that I am totally passionate about.'
                                                          John Cross, iSolon

A. 'My passions are people, rituals and behaviours, not products. Products are merely an output.'
                                                          Matt Marsh, Ideo

Q. On a day-to-day basis, what motivates you?

A. 'My motivations are creativity, making some money, fun and that's it! We also love what we do and people love our clients through a lot of the stuff that we do. Watching 3,000 kids running round a custom-made running track over burnt-out cars in the dark with a pumping sound system inside Battersea Power Station for Nike, for example.'
                                                          Mike Mathieson, Cake

A. 'My motivation is appalling customer service. Try travelling anywhere, for example. If you travel by plane, you're herded into seats (in which you can barely move) on a service that may, or may not, run on time. If you travel by train, it's usually dirty, there's often no seats at all and if there are delays (which invariably there are), you are not informed. So you try and travel by bus where you have even less room in your seat and the windows steam up. Is it surprising that everyone travels by car? I want to play a part in changing this.'
                                                          John Cross, iSolon

A. 'Making things better for people. There are so many dull, semi-functional things around; you only have to sneeze to find new challenges. We're particularly motivated by things that we call "standing waves" … things that have stayed the same for ages without anyone really questioning their contemporary relevance – bras are a good example!'
                                                          Richard Seymour, Seymour Powell

A. 'If something isn't going to be either useful, usable, delightful or best of all, all three, I have absolutely no motivation to be involved.'
                                                          Matt Marsh, Ideo

hey you

moment um

How do you develop your vision and creativity?

A. 'Two words sum up my creative force field, "user centred". The user is always at the centre of our thinking at Ideo – we believe in user-centred design, not universal design.

There is an issue, though, that consumers only know about the things they have experienced, which can cause problems in reviewing and researching a new concept. To solve this we look at opportunities in two ways. Explicit issues of which end users are aware we ask questions on; for latent issues of which end users are currently unaware we conduct observation exercises.

Creative solutions also often lie at the heart of problems themselves. One of the first things we do when faced with a problem is to redefine the problem statement. Our world is one of ambiguity and shades of colour, and too many times wrong diagnosis of a problem leads to poor solutions.'

Matt Marsh, Ideo

A. 'To think freely, one has to unburden the mind of all the usual noise that keeps intruding on useful thoughts developing.

Speaking personally, I can slip into a suitable contemplative state of mind without too much difficulty, perhaps walking through Hyde Park on my way to work, semi-dozing on a plane or soaking in the bath – much harder in front of a screen like right now.

Having got into the mood, the brain can either free scan, surfing data freestyle, or be consciously directed down a deliberate path. Creativity can result from either route, and sometimes the results can be quite unexpected. The brain is extremely data hungry and loves more and more material to play with.'

Richard James, eB2B PLC

How do you make your ideas happen?

A. 'We create contagious ideas by acting on them early and building on them collectively. Our area of expertise always relies on speed and spreadability. Our favourite saying is "Not everybody will go but everybody will know". We try to habitate in the centre of Word of Mouth (and Mouse!).'

Mike Mathieson, Cake

A. 'A mixture of self-belief, arrogance and bloody-mindedness. There are so many things that can kill a good idea that you often have to put on a suit of armour before going in to bat with a client. If something is better, it is worth defending
to the hilt.'   **Richard Seymour, Seymour Powell**

A. 'Share early and create an environment that is forgiving of mistakes. Also don't over-engineer – low-fidelity presentations are fine, and in some case the best solution if they transmit the passion and purpose of your idea and do it quickly. What do I mean by low fidelity? Paper, passion and loads of coloured pens.'   **Matt Marsh, Ideo**

Q. How do you create the right environment for nurturing your ideas?

A. 'By being open-minded and ripping all of the doors and glass out of the building. Understanding that the ideas from a 17-year-old are as potentially valid as your own. Involving everybody, going out to see and do stuff together and avoiding hierarchy and internal politics. Finally, and perhaps most importantly, turning off every fucking mobile phone in the room!'
                                    Mike Mathieson, Cake

A. 'All round our offices we have written out large "Defer judgement, encourage wild ideas, build on other people's ideas, stay focused and one conversation at
a time – it helps".'   **Matt Marsh, Ideo**

A. 'By setting up a company of like-minded individuals who care passionately about what they do. We put huge emphasis on the initial creative process, often leaving the pen (or mouse) on one side for days before committing to issues of form and function. Design is an intellectual process, it only becomes tangible when it leaves your wrist! We dream of what something should be
before we commit.'   **Richard Seymour, Seymour Powell**

'We (society) have a cultural ethic that requires us to be "busy" and another that suggests that ideas, if they are not followed through fully, are wasted.

Why? Only because most people are afraid to be wrong.

The problem is: it is difficult to look busy while you think. The modern office is a relic of the Industrial Revolution. it is designed for production, it is the wrong place to inspire creativity.

To have good ideas you have to have lots of ideas – and accept that many of them will be wrong. Nurturing these ideas is not the "busy" task that we set ourselves, it is that spare reading, the conversations you have with people about things you don't know anything about, it is that time spent in a coffee shop reading the local arts magazine or better yet, just staring into space and daydreaming.'

Mike Weber, The Ecademy

An ideapreneur in his natural habitat

Stuart Armstrong's vision and customer policy fit into the heart of the human economy. His company, Cookson's, is a fantastic example of a small business doing big business through the democratizing power of the internet.

Stuart decided he had to do something. He needed to take drastic action to keep his tool shop in Stockport alive and kicking. Half of all hardware shops were going out of business due to fierce competition from the big retailers like B & Q and Do It All. The future certainly did not look rosy.

So he locked himself away with his team to dissect the future of the business. They assessed their strengths and opportunities and the internet seemed to be screaming in their ears. Everyone was talking about it, it seemed to be perfect for selling specialized tools and Stuart could see it could benefit both suppliers and customers at the same time.

However, he made a key decision right at the very beginning – not to merely tack an internet front end on to their existing business and practise business as usual. Instead, he decided to change the whole way they handled the company.

'If the net is just tagged on to your existing business it won't work. You only gain the significant benefits if you change the entire way you conduct your business.'

In the existing shop they had 8,000 lines and 20 per cent of their orders were for unusual products and tools that they had to order specially. In their new model the customer's order was placed directly with a supplier who dealt directly with the customer, cutting out major chunks of the supply chain and reducing costs.

Suppliers could be confident that the customer was aware of their full range of products whereas in traditional tool shops, only the top ten per cent of a manufacturer's range is on display. After a series of internal and external site tests they finally went live. 'It was a bit frightening in the early stages. In our first month we only had four orders, this increased to 17 in the second month and we went on to double our turnover every quarter.

'Going on the internet has created a whole new business. We have 50,000 products on the web at the moment. It has had a massive effect and *Cooksons.com* has doubled the size of our original business. We generally receive a substantial number of orders a day and the result is that our turnover has soared.

'In addition to the swot analysis we did that long day in July two years ago we also did a "perfect world scenario". We decided our perfect world was a business where we didn't have to carry stock. We would use our experience and reputation for service to connect customers and suppliers. This is what we have achieved.

'A fundamental goal was that we didn't want to be drained of cash as the business grew.

'It's important in this kind of make-or-break situation to think out of the box and to set yourself clear targets. Our first year's figures were very close to what we had budgeted. We created a self-fulfilling prophecy based on detailed targets and weekly growth patterns. This gave us something definite to drive towards.

'Our reputation is based around specialist tools and just as with Amazon, first-time buyers probably log on to buy something they think they couldn't get anywhere else. After this first buy they may order something they could get from a local shop but by then, customer loyalty has been created through supplying unusual products and delivering them with extreme service.

'The pricing structure is also very different because our costs are reduced through operating on the net, we can further cut our prices and our bottom line is still healthier because of our reduced overheads.'

'The main reasons we've been successful are that we challenged our own and the market's preconceptions, went about everything in a logical way, and throughout, we believed it could work.'

Stuart Armstrong, Cookson's

chapter five
introducing mind play

Train to become a Master Ideapreneur

Mind Play is a full 52-week-a-year training programme constructed to meet the needs of future Ideapreneurs.

You provide the determination and we'll provide the training.

As with everything today, you can't just turn up and perform and expect a gold medal. Anyone training for a major sporting event, be it the Olympics, football, baseball or even marbles, now needs to train intensively, day-in day-out, for years. You need a training programme, a special diet, a personal trainer and specific objectives and targets to hit.

If you want to become great at generating ideas, it's no different, you have to train, and to help you, we have created a new and explosive fitness programme, Mind Play.

Mind Play is designed to exercise your mind and allow you to push back the boundaries of your thought processes. It will allow you to build on your strengths while compensating for your weaknesses and engendering complete flexibility in the way you think.

Mind Play trains the brain yet allows the mind to play.

Mind Play ain't heavy, so if it's not fun, it's not working!

'Brainwave studies show that true creativity, inspiration and even superb sporting or artistic performance involve a degree of training, teaching the brain to reach a higher level of achievement.'

Richard James, eB2B

How to pass 'go'

Mind Play helps you action *Hey You!*. It will help you to realize how prepared or otherwise you are to cope in an ideas world and show you the way forward for your skills development.

Mind Play introduces three main disciplines:

◆ **Imagineering Explosive Results:** concentrating on how to generate new ideas

◆ **Constructing Incendiary Campaigns:** designed to help you construct your messages

◆ **Exploding on the Scene:** focusing on making the most out of your ideas.

Each discipline has four stages, e.g. within 'Imagineering Explosive Results' the four stages are Prepare, Generate, Focus and Share.

Each stage contains a series of *mind steps* designed to build up your mind strength, with many mind steps featuring workouts. There are 52 workouts in all, one for each week of the year; each one should take around an hour. Workouts are the foundation of your journey towards Ideapreneurdom!

For the workouts to succeed, you need to make them fun. Involve colleagues and friends, record your thoughts and ideas in a simple but comfortable format, e.g. draw pictures, take photos, write poems or cut out clippings from newspapers and magazines. As your collection builds up you can review your developing skills.

To help you do this, you need to test your ideation strength and establish a benchmark to review your progress against.

It's time to tackle Master Class, our Explosive Thinking fitness test.

chapter six
master class

When the going gets tough

How fit is your mind? Are you up to completing a mental marathon, a half marathon, or even a brief jog round thinking man's park?

To help you find out whether you are up to it, we have constructed a simple diagnostic. If you have ever joined a gym you will have completed an initial workout to monitor your fitness level. A training programme is then created for you to build on your current fitness level and to help you achieve your specific objectives. This is exactly what our Master Class fitness test will do for you.

The benefits of completing master class

There are three important benefits:

◆ You will generate a picture of your current fitness level.

◆ It will help you focus on where you most need to practise.

◆ It will form the basis for generating improvement targets for you to review in the future.

Instructions

Follow each of the steps below to complete the diagnostic. Before charting your responses, look through the worked example (on page 49) to illustrate the recording and calculating process. Good luck!

1. Read and consider the 48 questions.

2. Photocopy the blank question sheets and the Idea Circle to record your answers on.

3. Record your answers to the questions on the three individual charts using scores between 1 and 4.

   1 = Never / Untrue / Poor

   2 = Sometimes / Fairly True / Below Average

   3 = Usually / Mostly True / Good

   4 = Always / Totally True / Excellent

4. Add the separate scores for each stage (e.g. Prepare or Generate) and divide your answer by four to calculate your average score for that stage. Do this calculation for all 12 stages.

5. Plot your 12 average scores on the Idea Circle and connect the points. This is your fitness profile.

   The higher the score on each axis, the closer you are to becoming a true Ideapreneur.

6. Using the results you have just calculated, set your own improvement targets. Looking at your fitness profile, decide which areas you wish to prioritize for immediate attention. Re-calculate your profile in three months' time.

Master class questions

Discipline 1: Imagineering explosive results

Prepare

◆ Do you know yourself inside out?

◆ Does your vision drive what you do?

◆ Do you manage mistakes and learn from them?

◆ Do you consciously clear your mind of old learning, ideas and habits?

Generate

◆ Do you connect unconnected ideas?

◆ Can you navigate between your analytical and creative mind space at will?

◆ Can you defer early judgement of ideas?

◆ Do you create more ideas than you can shake a stick at?

Focus

◆ Can you express your ideas in a clear and simple way?

◆ Is your life driven by clear goals?

◆ Do you step back from your ideas and look at them from different perspectives?

◆ Do you use clear criteria for judging when to jump straight in or when to take it step by step?

Share

◆ Do you share and test your ideas with a proven circle of influence?

◆ How good are you at stimulating others to think about your ideas?

- Do you pull value out of criticism?

- Do you recognize worthwhile contacts?

Discipline 2: Constructing incendiary campaigns

Build

- How good are you at applying logic to random lists?

- How do you rate your ability to turn ideas into stories?

- Do you prototype ideas so that people can really feel them?

- Do you harness the power of plain truth?

Brand

- Do you brand your idea from conception?

- Do you create your own language to communicate each idea?

- Do you place customer value at the heart of everything you do?

- Do you think local and global at the same time?

Recognize

- Do you cherish your relationships?

- Do you know all the people your friends know?

- If you have an idea, do you know whether to keep it in-house or look outside?

- Do you mine the knowledge within your customer and supplier base?

Score

- Do you treat chance meetings as pitch opportunities?

- Do you have a message for every audience?

- How well do you handle and build on difficult questions?

- Do you create 30-second messages for your ideas?

Discipline 3: Exploding on the scene

Perform

◆ How good are you at performing to time?

◆ Do you adjust your pitches to make them topical and local?

◆ Do you talk money with confidence?

◆ Do you feel comfortable handling humour?

Provoke

◆ How confident are you at breaking the performance rules for deliberate effect?

◆ Do you change your emotions at will during a pitch?

◆ Do you use props to change your performances into theatre?

◆ Do you try to out-pitch the best politician you've ever heard?

Grow

◆ Do you influence others with your passion and belief?

◆ Do people trust you?

◆ Is your dream reflected in the culture you have created?

◆ Do you form long-term partnerships with those you work among?

Aspire

◆ Do you use one idea as the platform for the next?

◆ Do you aspire to dominate your world?

◆ Do you stay humble even at times of great achievement?

◆ Can you galvanize people behind a crusade?

Example

Discipline 1: Imagineering explosive results

	1 *Never* *Untrue* *Poor*	2 *Sometimes* *Fairly True* *Below Average* *Average*	3 *Usually* *Mostly True* *Good*	4 *Always* *Totally True* *Excellent*
PREPARE				
Do you know yourself inside out?	✓			
Does your vision drive what you do?				✓
Do you manage mistakes and learn from them?		✓		
Do you consciously clear your mind of old learning, ideas and habits?			✓	
GENERATE				
Do you connect unconnected ideas?		✓		
Can you navigate between your analytical and creative mind space at will?			✓	
Can you defer early judgement of ideas?			✓	
Do you create more ideas then you can shake a stick at?				✓
FOCUS				
Can you express your ideas in a clear and simple way?	✓			
Is you life driven by clear goals?		✓		
Do you step back from your ideas and look at them from different perspectives?		✓		
Do you use clear criteria for judging when to jump straight in or when to take it step by step?			✓	
SHARE				
Do you share and test your ideas with a proven circle of influence?	✓			
How good are you at stimulating others to think about your ideas?			✓	
Do you pull value out of criticism?		✓		
Do you recognize worthwhile contacts?				✓

Fill in the chart as shown and then complete the following calculation for each power point.

PREPARE: 1 + 3 + 2 + 4 = 10   **GENERATE:** 2 + 3 + 3 + 4 = 12
10/4 = 2.5   12/4 = 3
FOCUS: 1 + 2 + 2 + 3 = 8   **SHARE:** 1 + 3 + 2 + 4 = 10
8/4 = 2   10/4 = 2.5

These results should then plotted on the corresponding axis on the Idea Circle – see example below.

Idea circle – example

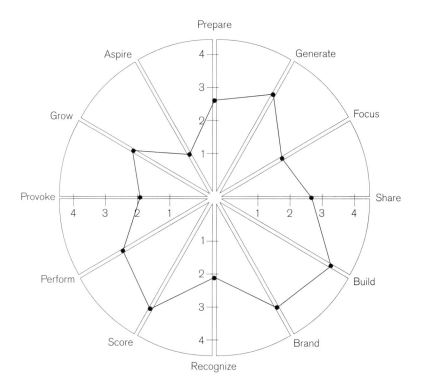

Discipline 1: Imagineering explosive results

	1	2	3	4
PREPARE				
Do you know yourself inside out?				
Does your vision drive what you do?				
Do you manage mistakes and learn from them?				
Do you consciously clear your mind of old learning, ideas and habits?				
GENERATE				
Do you connect unconnected ideas?				
Can you navigate between your analytical and creative mind space at will?				
Can you defer early judgement of ideas?				
Do you create more ideas than you can shake a stick at?				
FOCUS				
Can you express your ideas in a clear and simple way?				
Is your life driven by clear goals?				
Do you step back from your ideas and look at them from different perspectives?				
Do you use clear criteria for judging when to jump straight in or when to take it step by step?				
SHARE				
Do you share and test your ideas with a proven circle of influence?				
How good are you at stimulating others to think about your ideas?				
Do you pull value out of criticism?				
Do you recognize worthwhile contacts?				

Discipline 2: Constructing incendiary campaigns

	1	2	3	4
BUILD				
How good are you at applying logic to random lists?				
How do you rate your ability to turn ideas into stories?				
Do you prototype ideas so that people can really feel them?				
Do you harness the power of plain truth?				
BRAND				
Do you brand your idea from conception?				
Do you create your own language to communicate each idea?				
Do you place customer value at the heart of everything you do?				
Do you think local and global at the same time?				
RECOGNIZE				
Do you cherish your relationships?				
Do you know all the people your friends know?				
If you have an idea, do you know whether to keep it in-house or look outside?				
Do you mine the knowledge within your customer and supplier base?				
SCORE				
Do you treat chance meetings as pitch opportunities?				
Do you have a message for every audience?				
How well do you handle and build on difficult questions?				
Do you create 30-second messages for your ideas?				

Discipline 3: Exploding on the scene

	1	2	3	4
PERFORM				
How good are you at performing to time?				
Do you adjust your pitches to make them topical and local?				
Do you talk money with confidence?				
Do you feel comfortable handling humour?				
PROVOKE				
How confident are you at breaking the performance rules for deliberate effect?				
Do you change your emotions at will during a pitch?				
Do you use props to change your performances into theatre?				
Can you out-pitch the best politician you've ever heard?				
GROW				
Do you influence others with your passion and belief?				
Do people trust you?				
Is your dream reflected in the culture you have created?				
Do you form long-term partnerships with those you work among?				
ASPIRE				
Do you use one idea as the platform for the next?				
Do you aspire to dominate your world?				
Do you stay humble even at times of great achievement?				
Can you galvanize people behind a crusade?				

Idea circle

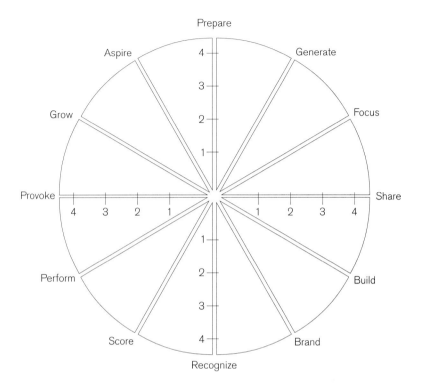

section two
imagineering explosive ideas

The first of the three Ideapreneur disciplines, 'Imagineering Explosive Ideas', takes you on a journey through the early stages of creating ideas.

IF I HAD FIVE HOURS TO

IF YOU HAVEN'T GO IT

CHOP DOWN A TREE

I'D SPEND FOUR HOURS

SHARPENING THE AXE

Abraham Lincoln

'Imagineering Explosive Ideas' is the foundation of becoming an Ideapreneur.

To that end you'll find that there is more in this section than the others, but mark my words, taking the time to think about exploding your ideas will be well worth the effort.

YOU CAN'T FLAUNT IT

hey you

moment um

chapter seven
prepare

Become an explosive thinker

Exude dedication and be mentally prepared. Develop motivation and the right environment to enhance your creativity. Know your values, create meaning for yourself, and take full responsibility for your own life. Be resolute and persistent always.

SIGNPOST

prepare

◆ Know your own uniqueness

◆ Vision express

◆ Willpower

◆ Be brave

◆ Learn to unlearn

◆ Nurture and nature

◆ Work ethic to ideas ethic

Welcome to prepare

'The will to win is important, but the will to prepare is vital.'

Joe Paterno

I don't know about you, but whenever I'm watching sports on TV I feel a tinge of regret, guilt even and a little despair. Sitting in the comfort of my home, in the deep recesses of the sofa, I can't help thinking, 'How the hell are these people performing all those amazing feats of the human body while I can barely summon up the energy and the inclination to go to the kitchen?'

My initial feelings, however, are often quickly assuaged by the realization that the superhuman beings parading about on the TV screen had to put in a massive amount of hard work, getting up at dawn every morning regardless of rain, hail or snow and pushing themselves to the limit.

They didn't wake up one day and discover they could do the Fosbury Flop or hit a tennis ball at a thousand miles an hour. These skills took years of preparation, commitment and dedication to perfect.

It may soothe our egos to know that maybe we could have done the same things if only we'd had the right inclination and training. It's even better to realize that even if it's too late to perfect our bodies, it is not too late to start training our minds. Right now, with a little Mind Play, anyone can train to become an Explosive Thinker.

'Chance favours only the prepared mind.'

Louis Pasteur

Talent spotting

Your mind may not have been picked out by a talent scout when you were five but you can still change the way you think now. If you want to use Mind Play to activate Explosive Thinking, the first step is to prepare your mind with a mental warm-up. The mind needs just as much care and attention as the body when it is about to work out. No one becomes a legend overnight, not even Ideapreneurs!

What you really, really want

How much do you want to make your ideas happen? Have you got the killer instinct? All the best Ideapreneurs have understood that to succeed you have to compete. Your idea must fight for space and, as an individual, you must champion both yourself and your idea.

If you want to be a star you have to believe your own twinkle, whoever or whatever tries to knock it out of you. Remember, nearly everyone who has achieved something great has first struggled to get there.

'I will prepare, and some day my chance will come.'   Abraham Lincoln

Prepare: Mind Step 1 Know your own uniqueness

'You have to expect things of yourself before you can do them.'   Michael Jordan

You have a choice.

If you want to cook a meal, you must either decide what you want to cook and buy the ingredients, or you can check out the fridge and decide what you can cook with the ingredients you've got. As with culinary delights, so with people.

When I was at school I had a friend who decided he wanted to become 'posh'. He went out, bought a waxed jacket, smart shoes and a cravat and hey presto he was re-born. He changed his name to something double barrelled, changed his voice till he was 'posher' than the Queen Mum and then he changed his friends. He changed himself so thoroughly that even his mother hardly knew him.

This is one way of getting to know yourself – decide who you want to be and become it. I couldn't do it myself but it worked for him – though he was rather an odd bloke. I guess you could say, if you are going to be a prat, at least be a complete one.

What he did have in his life, though, was clarity, and clarity is a great start. If you can discover what makes you unique, you can use it as the platform to build your ideas on.

If you know yourself, you can embrace uncertainty and build your own future.

Knowing yourself also allows you to take responsibility for your own life and career. No longer will you need to rely on your boss to think for you and pass ideas down the line.

So how do you create clarity without changing yourself to fit a stereotype?

Truly knowing yourself allows you to go where angels fear to tread and to keep going when everyone around you is screaming at you to stop. The key, though, is *to truly know yourself* and not just to think you do, otherwise you might end up invading Russia.

WORKOUT ONE

◆ Define your most unique qualities. List three things that you are doing to develop and two ways you can use them in your professional life.

◆ Ask two good friends what they admire about you. Repeat the exercise with two work colleagues. Compare and summarize their comments. How can you use this in developing your ideas?

◆ Decide who your two worst enemies are. (Everybody has some type of enemy, or at least people who aren't their greatest fans.) Imagine what they would say about you and check this with someone else, write it down and ask yourself 'Do they have a point?'

Prepare: Mind Step 2 Vision express

'Vision without action is a daydream. Action without vision is a nightmare.'
Japanese proverb

This is so true. I know there are a lot of quotes in this book, in fact there are a lot of quotes in most books, but this one is a cracker. I am lucky enough to have spent some time in Japan and it is the most awe-inspiring place in the world. If you want to generate more ideas, a visit to Japan is the next best thing to reading this book.

Anyway back to vision. I'm a bit of a vision fanatic – I'm afraid without vision I physically can't start something. If I had a pound for every meeting I've been in where, despite the spectacular challenge and possibilities of a project, the people involved have launched straight into mind-numbing minutiae and dreary little problem spotting, I would have more money than Bill Gates. Why oh why are some people so fascinated by the mundane?

If you want to be an Ideapreneur, never start something till you can see a glorious outcome. Soar like an eagle – see what can be done, not what can't be done.

The can't do bit comes later.

'My vision is not something separate. It's always with me like a warm envelope, an aura. It reminds me of the Ready Brek advert years ago, with the kid on his way to school in the middle of winter, kept warm by the cereal he has just eaten.'
John Cross, iSolon

It is also worth remembering that other people may see the same vision as you, but in a different light. When I was in Japan, I was told 'In Europe you take a week to make a decision and a year to make it work; in Japan we take a year to make a decision and a week to make it work.'

It's all a bit yin and yang!

Prepare: Mind Step 3 Willpower

'Success is the prize for those who stand true to their ideas!'

Josh S. Hinds

While writing this book and talking to as many Ideapreneurs as possible, it has become clear that there is one guiding principle to becoming a Master.

It is nothing to do with performing extraordinary feats, but everything to do with doing obvious things extraordinarily well.

Dedication should therefore be easy. It requires no special skills, just do the following:

◆ Yearn to be dedicated with all your heart.

◆ Stop doing all the rubbish things that are bogging you down.

◆ Dream your dream and believe in it totally.

◆ Surround yourself with talented people.

◆ Don't be afraid of hard work.

◆ Never tolerate anything second rate.

Follow these rules and you will master willpower and dedication. Then you'll be ready to kick some ideas arse!

Inspiration not perspiration

'To succeed ... you need to find something to hold on to, something to motivate you, something to inspire you.'   Tony Dorsett

There are too many exciting things going on these days to continue in a boring, uninspiring job. The other day I was presenting about life in the human economy and afterwards half the people there were talking about how uninspired they were by what they were doing. If that is true of you – move on for goodness sake.

You have only one life, so use it. Either join a company whose vision, values and virtues inspire you or, better still, start your own.

Whatever you do, never join a company until they can articulate their vision, values and virtues to you with utter passion and belief.

Every choice you make

You may think your life is one long continuum, but in fact life is a series of moments, opportunities and choices. It is at the moments of choice that you shape your own destiny.

If you want to keep making the right choices, you need to focus on your Explosive Idea and keep it front of mind. Every choice you make takes your idea a step nearer or a step further away from your dream. Use your willpower to ensure that every choice you make brings you closer to your vision.

Determined dreaming

'The difference between the impossible and the possible lies in a man's determination.'   Tommy Lasorda

Dreaming is amazing. Determined dreaming is profoundly productive.

Go for it!

Ideapreneurs always want to make a difference, they want to change the world and that involves winners and losers. It's important to remember that:

Winning becomes a habit, but so does losing.

If you want to win big, don't be a loner – influence the people around you and create a whole winning team. Working clever is better than working hard, but if you can combine the two and work as a team then the world is your oyster.

'The difference between a successful person and others is not a lack of strength, not a lack of knowledge, but rather a lack of will.'

Vincent T. Lombardi

Prepare: Mind Step 4 Be brave

'Leap before you look.' The Fourth Room

This was the motto of The Fourth Room where I used to work. The thought behind it is very simple – with the world changing as fast as it is, you have to take action first and sort out the fine print later.

If you want to get ahead of the pack, this is rapidly becoming the only way to think. Be brave – what have you got to lose? Apart from the house, the partner, the car, the dog, the pension. Only kidding, let's be serious for a moment – you can always get another dog!

The reality is that, in nine cases out of ten, when people are scared of taking action one of two things is true:

◆ *either* there is no reason to be scared, just the propagation of ancient old wives tales, in which case you should just get on with it

◆ *or* the environment you are working in is genuinely so censorious that it punishes people who try their best but fail. In this case you are better off out of there. No one needs this sort of nonsense these days.

When I first joined BT everybody told me what I couldn't do, who I couldn't talk to, what was never done, indeed what one was never to mention. The list of don'ts was endless. What nobody told me, though, was what I actually could do. In a company where everybody seemed to have been working there for ten years or more, this could have been a bit daunting.

Not a bit of it; for a hot-blooded young marketer straight from the retail industry it was like dying and going to heaven. At last I could do anything I wanted. I made friends with sales (seen as a crime by the rest of marketing), spoke to directors and even said what I was thinking, I set up loads of initiatives and communicated with anyone who would listen. It was a truly marvellous time and none of the dire warnings I was given by the dusty old guard were worth a thing.

Never worry about a few mistakes – the only terminal mistake is not to try. Failure and mistakes are as much part of life as eating, drinking and falling in love. If you are not doing it, you are probably not living. For the brave there is always life after failure, again and again and again.

Two key things are worth mentioning:

◆ It is not the making of mistakes that is important, it is the learning from them that follows.

◆ You don't only need to learn from your *own* mistakes, you need to learn from the mistakes of others as well. This is one of the things that distinguishes high-achievers from other mortals. They learn as much as they can from everyone because they are innately curious. They seek out people they admire and get close to them. They ask them about their successes and are just as eager to hear about their failures.

There is nothing wrong with making mistakes as long as you are learning from them, but as a strategy for achieving greatness in its own right it won't work. By the time you have made every mistake you need to make to be a premier league player, you will be well over 100 and may even be heading for a double century!

'There is a microscopically fine line between being brilliantly creative and acting like the most gigantic idiot on earth. So what the hell, leap!'
Cynthia Heimel

Another company I have been working with is called What If. They wrote a book recently called *How to Start a Creative Revolution at Work* and, like me, they have a strong belief in corporate values and feature them at large in their corporate brochures.

These are their values:

◆ passion

◆ bravery

◆ freshness

◆ action

◆ love.

And what do they have to say about bravery?

'The original meaning of bravery or courage is to speak your mind with all your heart. Follow your gut, don't be afraid to make a fool of yourself.'
What If

Sounds good to me.

Being brave in terms of being creative is all about overriding your basic desire to run away from wild ideas. When was the last time you had butterflies in your tummy because of a creative idea?

'It's lack of faith that makes people afraid of meeting challenges, and I believed in myself.'
Muhammad Ali

At crunch time, instincts will prevail. So you need to change your attitude to risk taking. If you get your self-belief right, you should be ready, willing and able to take off from your comfort zone, to embrace uncertainty and thrive through instability.

'The best ideas come from taking chances and going with your instinct. Take a risk, be the first, do something breathtaking.'

Mike Mathieson, Cake

Bravery with ideas means exposing your deepest thoughts and inner feelings. You have to be prepared to expose your most sacred beliefs in your ideas and be prepared to stand by them through criticism and derision.

'It is not because things are difficult that we do not dare; it's because we do not dare that things are difficult.'   Seneca

Bravery is not stupidity – you always need to listen to feedback from other people, but remember that their views are not always right. It costs you nothing to listen, but it may cost you everything if you lose your faith.

WORKOUT THREE

◆ Think of the last time you leapt before you looked. What three good things came of it? Identify another opportunity to leap into.

◆ When was the last time you made a mistake and what did you learn from it? Write down two ways you can use this learning.

◆ Identify two mistakes made by other people that you have learnt from and two mistakes you could have learnt from but haven't. What are you doing to avoid making the same mistakes yourself?

Prepare: Mind Step 5 Learn to unlearn

'Either you think, or else others have to think for you and take power from you, pervert and discipline your natural tastes, civilise and sterilise you.'

F. Scott Fitzgerald

That tells you!

Unknow today what you won't need tomorrow

Unknowing and the notion of an ignorance economy are not half as crazy as they sound. They're about positively updating your mind and being open to new ideas and new experiences. Unknowing is as much about receiving new ideas as it is about throwing out old ones. To stay receptive the brain needs to be constantly activated and refreshed. It needs to restructure and to reassess.

Some old ideas may just need a tweak, some may need a complete makeover and some need to be chucked out. It's all about different thinking.

Today the average person has to rebuild their knowledge base from scratch every three or four years.

Incredible in itself, but not only do you need to churn your knowledge, you need to churn your personal operating systems as well.

To put this into context, think of your head as an office for a moment. Running an office these days you need to constantly upgrade your PCs, buy new software, develop new systems, bin loads of paper, become mobile and embrace video conferencing, all in a day's work. Compare the average office environment and working practices of five years ago to those of today and it is easy to see why it is time to upgrade your thinking!

In today's world you can't rely on others to manage this for you. If you are not personally managing your own head, it won't be long before you have a derelict brownfield site on your hands!

This is actually quite scary. Previous generations never had to unload themselves like we do and it is not a skill many of us are set up to handle.

But it is far from all bad. At The Fourth Room we used to talk about not knowing as a virtue. If you were working with a client in a sector where you were experienced, you passed the project on to someone else in the team. It gave you the opportunity to say, 'I know, but I know a man who doesn't.'

And there is another silver lining to the not-knowing cloud.

The rapid churn of relevant knowledge and trends in thinking means that re-entry into work or career switching is easier now than ever before.

The job market has never been more open. If you present strongly at interview and possess an inquiring mind, bravery and confidence, you can out-perform people already doing related jobs.

WORKOUT FOUR

◆ Make a list of three people who you allow to do your thinking for you. Identify anything you are doing as a result that doesn't fit your personal vision. What two actions can you take to stop this happening?

◆ Think of an old idea that you could turn inside out. Consider three changes to the idea and three new applications.

◆ In the spirit of unlearning, spotlight three things you no longer need to know and three things you should stop doing.

Prepare: Mind Step 6 Nurture and nature

However personally motivated they are and however naturally talented, most Ideapreneurs need to nurture their talent in an

Ideapreneurial environment, one that is ripe for ideas, creativity and original thinking.

What is the right environment?

From a factual stance the right environment usually encompasses the physical environment, spiritual atmosphere and the personal dynamics within the workplace.

Imagination, a company in London, prides itself on, yes you've guessed it, its imagination. They work out of the 'imagination building' and I have to say being in there does inspire one to think. They are by no means unique, however – most creative companies have offices, some even call them homes (pretentious moi), designed to inspire those that work there.

So what are these offices actually like?

Like most things connected to ideas and the generation of ideas there isn't only one answer, though some features seem to recur quite a lot. Here is a quick summary of some of the most popular and some of the more esoteric trends being trailed by professional idea buffs.

Colour

This is one way to make people think differently and one that, as a painter, I personally like. We've just painted the Team Murray walls a delicate shade of Wedgwood blue. Do some research first, though – colour magic needs to be understood.

Whiteness

As an alternative to colour, white is incredibly popular with 'creatives'. Minimalism is a safe option and won't upset your clients, but there is a massive difference between designer-white yen space and just splashing a tin of brilliant white on the walls.

Openness

Ideas are for sharing, so open is generally considered the way to go, but don't be pushed into this if you don't feel it will work for you. With people being people, sometimes they work better apart from each other. Maybe you are innately anti-social, so don't be bullied into sitting on someone's lap.

Ideas don't like to be cramped, they don't like to see the same things or the same people every day.

Homeliness

This one's my favourite, as there are very few 'office' spaces I particularly like.

At Team Murray we chucked our desks into the skip, and replaced them with settees and big round tables so that we could spread out communally, very King Arthur. To make our space totally personal and involving, we gave colleagues a 'pot' of money for buying furniture and delightful objects of their choice.

Team members have even started stripping out their homes of their favourite things and bringing them to work because they enjoy them more at work than at home!

Informality

Informality works. Shabby, on the other hand, is still just shabby.

Hospitality

If you want to work with ideas then be hospitable. Just as at parties where everyone congregates in the kitchen – you can make this happen at work too. Turn the place where you work into a Mecca for clients, friends, relatives and partners and watch the ideas flow. Glorious food and drink are the lifeblood of great ideas.

Urban chic

Safe but effective.

Funky

Becoming more and more popular – anything goes.

Historic

This is the way to go if you want real idea cache. Work in a castle, or the former home of Oscar Wilde. Let the ghosts of past glories be your muse. Also works a treat with clients. (If you're in a brand new office space where history is a little lacking, try coming up with a story for the foundations.)

Zonal

Split your workplace up into totally different zones with wickedly different feels. Remember there is never only one right way.

Greenfield

Move out of the towns and cities into the countryside. Let the field be with you!

Hot desking

Approach with caution, but it can work.

Home working

As above, one person's convenience is another's lonely hell.

Cheap and cheerful

Don't waste money – the most inspirational things can be quite cheap.

Playroom

Very much the fashion in LA, silly job titles, off-the-wall jobs, adults behaving like kids, etc. Not my cup of tea, but who knows?

WORKOUT FIVE

◆ Start to consider the role colour plays in your creative inspiration. Find a book about the power of colour and read it. List two ways to use colour in your workplace positively.

◆ Decide what two things you can change at work, however large or small, to make your environment more creative.

◆ Arrange to personally cook a meal for a client or key contact.

◆ Think about the people that work with you. What two things can you do to give them enough space to think? Discuss these with them.

Prepare: Mind Step 7 Work ethic to ideas ethic

If you want to be a Master Ideapreneur, stop thinking about how hard you work and concentrate purely on the power of your ideas.

Ideapreneurs are first and foremost just that – Ideapreneurs. It's time to eat sleep and breathe the infinite possibilities of your imagination.

Believe that you are a creative engine and that the world is truly lucky to have you. See ideas wherever you go, think of everyone you meet as part of your winning team.

Now you're ready!

WORKOUT SIX

◆ How significant a role do your ideas play in your day-to-day life? Create a log over a couple of days to chart how significantly your ideas feature in your daily thoughts. Include references to your dreams too.

PREPARE

- The will to prepare is vital.

- It's never too late to change the way you think.

- Know yourself to build your own future.

- A dream without vision is a nightmare.

- Dreaming is amazing. Determined dreaming is profoundly productive.

- Do obvious things extremely well.

- Transform your work ethic into an ideas ethic.

TRIGGER

If you have five hours to chop down a tree, spend four of them sharpening the axe.

generate

Unleash the power of thought

The essence of creativity, sources of inspiration and how to produce killer ideas with unconventional thinking.

SIGNPOST

generate

◆ Flex your creative muscles

◆ Develop a sixth sense

◆ Silence the voices

◆ Get angry

◆ Fecundorious

◆ Live in two worlds

◆ Imagineer the future

Welcome to generate

However much has been written about creativity, it clearly isn't enough or it's not good enough, because consistently generating exciting new ideas is still one of the most exacting tasks in life today.

In searching for the Holy Grail of creativity, we decided to seek out and talk to people who make their living directly from generating and developing new ideas.

This was a big mistake – in fact, it was a huge mistake. The more you ask these guys about the secret of their creativity, the more shrouded in mystery the whole thing becomes. After a while of listening to various tales of smoke and mirrors (more smoke, actually, than mirrors) you are left with the distinct impression that most of these professional ideas people are asking themselves the same questions, in a desperate attempt to maintain the flow of their own inspiration.

Actually to be fair, having said the whole exercise was a big mistake, we did meet some fascinating individuals and enjoy some wild evenings.

And did we actually learn anything? Well, yes we did. On a few things, the majority of professional 'creatives' seem to agree.

Generating ideas is not a process that can be institutionalized but it can be fostered both on an individual and team basis.

Idea generation is more about attitude than skill. There are some highly effective creative-thinking models like Edward de Bono's *Lateral Thinking* and Tony Buzan's *Mind Mapping*, which if you haven't read already, you should. Ultimately, however, these are only helpful tools.

Look at it this way – having a great big power tool doesn't make you a DIY expert, but on the other hand, a bad workman always blames his tools.

As explored earlier, your immediate environment is important in generating ideas, and this is especially so for people working in teams. You may have your best ideas in the bath, the South of France or even a smoky room in south-east London, but if you want ideas to flow, go where you feel inspired and make your immediate environment work for you. Me, I find sitting in a jacuzzi, overlooking powder-white sand and turquoise-blue sea while sipping champagne can be quite inspirational.

Sharing is also important. A mix of arrogance and humility works well in an Ideapreneur. You need to be arrogant enough to believe you can produce sheer brilliance but humble enough to share your ideas with friends. Learn to completely listen and to be open to taking your friends' feedback into account.

Imagination breeds imagination – share good ideas and you'll end up with an Ideapreneurs' Mexican Wave.

What else did we learn? One important thing – everyone can be creative. It is not the exclusive domain of the advertising or marketing industries. Regardless of age, job or anything else, if you develop the right attitude and do the right things you too can be extraordinarily creative.

So what is generate about?

'Generate' is not a universal panacea for idea generation but hopefully it can help both teams and individuals release the creativity that is already there.

As creativity is more about attitude than 'being creative', start thinking about creativity as something you are, rather than something you do. Alternatively, think of it as a way to live rather than a way to enhance life. By doing this, you will be well on your way to becoming an Ideapreneur.

Or to put it in luvvie speak:

Generating ideas is intelligence having fun and 'Generate' aims to bring together art and business in a way that constantly re-expresses the human spirit, to provide a bounty of inspiration. More than anything else, creativity is the search for new meanings, from 'Developing a sixth sense', to 'Getting angry', let us guide you on your creative pilgrimage.

Take your pick!

One thing you can be sure of – at this very moment, someone, somewhere is creating the next big thing: designing a new iMac, writing the next Harry Potter or creating a thrilling new customer experience, changing their own and other people's lives for ever.

Tomorrow, it could be you!

Generate: Mind Step 1 Flex your creative muscles

You've got a blank sheet of paper and you want to get creative. Where do you start? How do you flex your creative muscles?

You accept that creative energy is innate within all of us but some people seem to know how to release it better than others. Maybe it's time to try to think differently, to look at how you currently seek inspiration and change the way you're doing it.

Every time you wake up, check the alarm clock, have a shower, get dressed, eat your breakfast, catch the train to work, or however you start your day, you are acting out a ritual. If the train timetable changes, you adjust your ritual to cope and still get to work on time. Being able to do this is actually pretty useful, and if we go back a few years it was critical to survival.

The brain has strong natural tendencies that battle with your creative urges on a daily basis. It automatically sorts out and integrates new thoughts, experiences and ideas against existing data, to fit known patterns. The down side, however, is that it fosters stale thinking.

But imagine waking up and saying, 'Blow this for a game of soldiers, I'm off.' Get out your passport, pack a few clothes and go straight down to the airport. One minute Wapping, next minute Radjistan. No more routine, no more happy comfort zone, only life-changing new experiences.

It's a great idea but not always practical, so if you can't transport your body, transport your mind. Aim to overwhelm the traditional constraints that allow your own mind to impose on the way you want to think. These need to be overcome so you can create brand new categories and dimensions of thoughts and ideas.

One way to do this is to transport yourself to a completely different world and start to think about the issue the way you would if you lived in that world. Choose any world you like, outer space, the Stone Age, a tropical rain forest, the playboy mansion, the wackier the better. Make the illusion as real as possible and if you are in a group, try actually using props to spice up the idea. Knock back all thinking that would not fit your assumed world, but don't get too anal and forget the fun.

Having a laugh is a great way to get ideas going

When I worked at The Fourth Room in London we were very conscious of these things. Instead of having an office we had a 'home' complete with a dining room, a housekeeper, at-home dinners and amazing breakfasts for friends.

Where we worked was very much part of who we were and what we did. Each room in the house had a very different feel, from the relaxed Georgian sitting room to the 'Fourth Room' itself after which the company was named. This room was completely white, walls, floor, rugs everything; this was the room of 'un-knowing'. When you went in this room you were expected to leave all preconceptions at the door.

And it really did make a difference. Both team members and guests enjoyed being there, they felt at home and creativity flowed. The Fourth Room 'home' was all about an alternative approach to thinking.

The comparison with BT where I also worked could not have been more stark. Despite spending a fortune on updating their accommodation, BT managed to drive out any sense of flair or individualism. Their buildings all around the country were fitted out in near-identical mid-European grey. What colour is that, you ask? It's the same colour as your average Euro technocrat living in Brussels.

Teamwork vanished and creativity was replaced by conformity. It is extremely hard to embrace fresh thinking in Dull City Arizona.

'The modern office is the wrong place to inspire creativity. Somehow you must make your desk your sanctuary, your amusement park. Throw a party, take the office ice skating, encourage your staff to do their paperwork in the park – get people to relate to their work as a fun and integral part of their lives.'
Mike Weber

Your thinking should involve the juxtaposition of apparently unrelated thoughts and feelings and at its heart should be the ability to unlearn. At a recent conference I attended, they talked about the 'ignorance economy' in a positive light. Ignorance can be bliss if the alternative is constraining the imagination.

Having the idea in the first place is only stage one. All of the world's best ideas have faced massive and immediate opposition from those who thought they knew better.

So if creativity is about attitude not just skill, what is the right attitude for enabling your thinking to develop?

Continual curiosity, fuelled by happy ignorance or healthy not knowing, wrapped in role play and dressed with a coulis of creative environment.
Perfect.

Generate: Mind Step 2 Develop a sixth sense

'Wit is the sudden marriage of ideas which before their union were not perceived to have any relation.' Mark Twain

It seems that creative people have a kind of sixth sense. They have a knack of absorbing the world around them and representing it again in a whole new light.

Cultivating this creative sixth sense will enable you to harmonize external influences for internal Feng Shui.

Developing your own sixth sense is all about recognizing creative stimuli and keeping your sensors on alert at all times to act upon sources of inspiration.

Getting from A to B is all well and good, but a gentle meander may be a hell of a lot more productive for your mind. When you take the time to wander, you let your mind appreciate your surroundings not only as a means to an end but as vital stimulus.

Sixth sense is about building new thought bridges. Breakthrough creativity happens at the crossroads of unconnected spheres of thought. It's about unleashing the power of the impossible.

To generate ideas you need to think like a poet, think metaphorically and comparatively.

Be intuitive – don't just think about work at work. This doesn't mean you have to think about work all the time, but rather just be aware of ways in which you can merge and incorporate different areas of your life – fashion, art, architecture, music and, of course, nature.

hey you

momentum

Generate: Mind Step 3 Silence the voices

'An idea that is not dangerous is not worthy of being called an idea at all.'
Elbert Hubbard

How often have brilliant ideas been dismissed by misguided judgement applied far too early? To enable creativity, you must fight the voice of judgement and ambush internal criticism.

Stanford Graduate School of Business professor Michael Ray has built his whole life around this concept. He has taught the groundbreaking course 'Personal Creativity in Business' since 1979. His protégés include Steve Jobs, founder of Apple, Jeff Skoll, VP of strategic planning at eBay, Gary Marenzi, president of international television at Paramount, and Joanne Ernst, female tri-athlete. He argues that creativity exists within everyone and is only suppressed by the 'voice of judgement'.

One way to defer judgement is to relive your childhood and forget all about risk management. Young children have no fear of ridicule when they are playing, they are the richest source of fantastical thinking I have ever encountered. I have two boys, George aged eight and Henry four; already they have taught me so much.

WORKOUT EIGHT

◆ Explain your job or idea to a child under ten. First of all, can you get them to understand? And second, record what fresh insights and perspectives they bring.

Generate: Mind Step 4 Paint your world

Truly great artists can absorb and regurgitate the world around them better than anyone. Artists like Monet, Van Gogh, Picasso and Matisse, had such talent that they gave the world new eyes to see with. These guys were world-class Ideapreneurs!

Can you close your eyes and paint your idea? Can you see it as a cameo, a panorama or a Cubist three-dimensional masterpiece? Can you physically capture your idea, in whatever media, to delight and astound yourself and your audience?

WORKOUT NINE

◆ As a basis take either something you are currently working on or an idea that you are still developing, and physically bring it to life.

Use anything you like such as paint, fabric, pens, paper, magazine cuttings, etc. to create a powerful, visual image for your idea. Make sure it mirrors the picture in your head.

Generate: Mind Step 5 Get angry

Don't be afraid to act on your frustrations and follow through on things that really annoy you.

Have you ever got to the stage where you think, 'Nothing's ever going to change unless I bloody well do it myself'?

Anger is a powerful catalyst for creating ideas – when you use it constructively!

Generate: Mind Step 6 Fecundorious

'If you want to have a great idea, have lots of ideas.' Linus Pauling

What does fecundorious mean? You won't find it in any dictionary because I made it up, but if fecund means fertile, fecundorious must mean gloriously fertile. And this is just what you need to be.

Being an Ideapreneur isn't about having one big idea, it's about having loads of ideas and then building them into the new wonders of the modern world.

Capitalizing on enlightened trial and error is a core competence in the seasoned entrepreneur.

Producing new ideas faster than acorns grow on oak trees is integral to both business and personal revolutions. Most Ideapreneurs know this and they relish churning out their ideas. By producing loads of ideas and allowing the runts to die off quickly, they allow winning ideas to grow fast with more tender love and care and thrive in the marketplace before the competition can catch up.

'Daring ideas are like chessmen moved forward; they may be beaten, but they may start a winning game.' Goethe

◆ When was the last time you were really angry at work? Write down how it made you feel and what you did about it. Did you harness your anger to solve the problem?

◆ Brainstorm 25 ideas related to something you are working on. Can you use any of them?

Generate: Mind Step 7 Live in two worlds

I was once chatting with Matt Kingdom from What If about the importance of recognizing that we live in two worlds – the analytical world and the creative world. He believes it's essential to feel comfortable in both worlds and be able to navigate between the two if you want to start your own creative revolution.

Why be pigeon-holed in one world when there are two to choose from? Learn to float effortlessly across from one to the other.

I have to say, though, that in my experience most of the people I know often visit half a dozen worlds, mainly uninhabited.

Generate: Mind Step 8 Imagineer the future

You can either forecast your future, or let it rain down upon you. Forecasting your future is about knowing how to maximize all opportunities in a constantly changing ideas world. We are not talking crystal balls here – the important signs are probably there if you look. Keep one ear to the ground for rumbles of opportunity and have eyes in the back of your head for any sparks of inspiration.

'Opportunities ... made these men successful, and their outstanding ingenuity made that opportunity known to them.'

Machiavelli

Pre-empting the ebbs and flows, not only of the market but of the world in general, is vitally important. If you can get even a glimmer of how people and environments are changing, then you're flying high.

GENERATE

◆ Be prepared to lose the routine.

◆ You can't embrace fresh thinking in Dull City Arizona.

◆ Ambush the voice of early judgement.

◆ Take your ideas to the park.

◆ Quiz your ideas with the voice of a child.

◆ Explode your ideas in paint.

◆ If you want Explosive Ideas, have loads of ideas.

TRIGGER

Imagination breeds imagination – create your own Ideapreneurs' Mexican Wave.

chapter nine
focus

analyze prioritize simplify

Action your ideas through analysis,
prioritization and simplifications.

SIGNPOST

focus

◆ What a goal

◆ Creative dissection

◆ Look outside

◆ Walk before you run

◆ Stick to your knitting

◆ Simplicity itself

Welcome to focus

It is great having loads of groundbreaking dreams and visions, but they are no use to anyone languishing in your brain or luxuriating on endless dog-eared post-its!

Equally there is no point putting hours of effort into an idea if you don't have clear goals and objectives.

Focus: Mind Step 1 What a goal

Without goals you are a mere puff of wind.

Lack of goals causes more misery in life than almost anything else. Have you ever wondered why so many incredibly wealthy people are so miserable? It's because they lack purpose in their lives.

If you ever meet a fairy who wants to grant you a wish, my advice is don't go for beauty or wealth – they are not all they are cracked up to be. Instead go for hard work and a clear goal.

As any serious athlete will tell you, without explicit goals you don't have a chance in hell of any major success. Being an Ideapreneur requires the same degree of focus. Set goals to cover all aspects of your exploding idea.

'Setting a goal is not the main thing. It is deciding how you will go about achieving it and staying with that plan.'

Tom Landry

Explosive Thinkers captain their own ideas and if you have already set clear goals and targets you will be well placed. Now you need to learn how to monitor your performance.

Make sure the goals you have set stay front of mind. Set them out in a way that is clear and attractive to look at and carry them with you at all times. Every morning before you start any other work, look at your goals and ask yourself how you are getting on. Are you making progress or is it time to move your goals on?

Remember that goalposts can be moved if you do it consciously and for good reasons; after all, they're not the ten commandments.

WORKOUT TWELVE

◆ List your five most important personal and career goals with precise timescales and measures. Capture your goals on a postcard that you can carry with you.

◆ Everyone needs a mentor — choose one for yourself. Ask them if they will consent to this and review your goals with them.

Focus: Mind Step 2 Creative dissection

'Problems cannot be solved at the same level of awareness that created them.' Albert Einstein

Put your ideas under the microscope. This doesn't mean rationalizing or diluting your more extreme ideas or forsaking the liberation and exhilaration of creativity, but it does mean an almost scientific deconstruction and then reconstruction of your ideas.

Shift your perspective and apply a kind of scientific inquiry to your creativity. Forensic science meets blue-sky thinking.

After all the time, energy and love you've put into your idea it can be hard to ask searching questions, but if you don't give your idea the Spanish Inquisition then I guarantee there'll be someone close at hand who's happy to do it for you.

You can't always do this on your own – sometimes you are going to need help. Surround yourself with people you trust from all areas of your life and start dissecting. Question them hard about your idea, make them look at your idea from multiple angles. Think about the most determined political interviewer you have ever heard or seen and take a leaf out of their book. Make Jerry Springer or Jeremy Paxman look shy and retiring. Push the same question five times and compare the answers.

'If you push people out of their comfort zone they stop saying what they think you want to hear.

Disorientate them with combative questions and you are likely to hear some startling insights.

It's like reverse brainwashing.'   Annalese Banbury

You might say that if you really want to get to the bottom of things you have to strip-search your idea. Be brave and brace yourself – this type of examination can hurt. But don't worry, in the long term it will hurt your competition a lot more than it hurts you.

WORKOUT THIRTEEN

◆ Identify four different angles from which to look at one of your ideas. Utilize them.

◆ You need to push those people helping you to dissect your ideas out of their comfort zone. What three things can you do to make them less comfortable, get under the skin of your idea and avoid the platitudes?

Focus: Mind Step 3 Look outside

'You can tune your instinct for market timing by living and breathing among it, by reading the papers, going to the cities, listening to people and communicating.'   Mike Mathieson, Cake

Be a jujitsu master

The traditional Japanese martial art jujitsu concentrates on using your opponent's force as your defence. By examining your world you can take advantage of other people's momentum and capitalize on past and present successes, failures and mistakes. There is so much information out there you'd be a fool not to use it.

'Study the deeds of great men ... examine the reasons for their victories and for their defeats.'

Machiavelli

You need to know not only yourself but also the world of your predecessors and rivals. Although creativity and ideas can come from within, nothing is entirely and purely original. Being aware and observant are vital skills for an Ideapreneur.

'Originality is nothing but judicious imitation.'

Voltaire

'If you know the enemy and know yourself, you need not fear the result of a hundred battles. If you know yourself but not the enemy, for every victory gained you will also suffer a defeat. If you know neither the enemy nor yourself, you will succumb in every battle.'

Sun Tzu

WORKOUT FOURTEEN

◆ Compile three separate lists, covering your top five peers, rivals and competitors.

What are the key strengths of each?

Taking each strength in turn, build them into something that you can use yourself.

Focus: Mind Step 4 Walk before you can run

All ideas are equal but some are a lot more equal than others. The ability to prioritize between good ideas can be difficult to maintain when over-enthusiasm takes hold. But however much you may want to do things, biting off more than you can chew only leads to choking and death.

Personally I find this step quite hard to deal with – I have a clear vision, other people are excited, I know the windows of opportunity are limited and I want to do it all, but it's a harsh fact of life that in many cases there is no other answer than walking before you can run.

I have a good friend called Mike Reid who until recently was a financial trader. He talks about the way traders need to create their own capital through trading before they can invest further. Ideas have to be proved in a step-by-step way before they are invested in.

Categorically, though, this isn't always the answer, because if you adhere to it religiously you will miss out on the biggest opportunities. But think of this way as your default setting and you may save yourself a lot of pain and anguish.

Making the right call on whether to walk before you can run or alternatively leap before you can look is where experience cuts in. You will need to try it both ways a few times and see when each works best for you.

WORKOUT FIFTEEN

◆ Look at two opportunities that you faced recently and consider, should you have leapt before you looked or walked before you ran?

◆ What criteria did you use to decide? Were these the correct criteria and what criteria can you use in the future?

Focus: Mind Step 5 Stick to your knitting

'If you want to be good in business, find out what you're good at, keep on doing it, adapt it and do it some more.'   Mike Reid

It may be boring, but if you look at many of the most successful people in business, they become extremely good at one thing and then rely on finding new opportunities to do it.

Learning curves are messy and slow so only go down one when you have to.

This doesn't mean being less creative, innovative or any less of an Ideapreneur, but it does mean working wise. Putting parameters around your creativity often forces you to be more creative and it makes you avoid taking the easy way out.

WORKOUT SIXTEEN

◆ Looking only at your immediate work project, brainstorm three ideas that you can apply straightaway.

Focus: Mind Step 6 Simplicity Itself

'Simplifying your ideas creates a clear strategic path to execution, unmuddled by too many distractions.'   Mike Mathieson, Cake

Simple ideas are fast and slippery and ideas that spread fastest win.

◆ Start with a simple idea – they are generally more likely to work.

◆ Pull out simple benefits for your end users.

◆ Provide simple reasons why those you want to involve should get involved.

- Create an incisive credo.

- Communicate often.

FOCUS

- Without goals you are a mere puff of wind.

- Forecast your own future or let it rain on you.

- Dissect your idea.

- Study everything around you as hard as you study yourself.

- Pace your ideas.

- Do only what you are best at.

- The simplest ideas are the most slippery.

TRIGGER

Don't review your idea with the same mind that created it.

chapter ten
share

no mind is an island

Once your idea is fully formed it's time to share it among a supportive crowd – the myth of the lone entrepreneur is being slowly eroded.

SIGNPOST

share

- ◆ Compose a circle of influence

- ◆ Recharge your batteries

- ◆ Take the flak

Welcome to share

Nobody is as clever as everybody.

This sentiment is now beginning to be fully appreciated and even deep in the shadows of Silicon Valley, it seems it's the end of an era for the lonesome frontiersmen.

Share explores the exchange and cross-fertilization of ideas and it looks at how Explosive Thinkers relish the chance to show and tell. They realize there's no better way to start an explosion and detect whether an idea has that killer touch than when you have people gossiping about it.

Explosive Thinking revolves around sharing, communicating and networking ideas. To some extent networking as a phrase has picked up some negative associations of schmoozing and gossip, but now is the time to brush these aside and make networking your way of life.

Everyone should be doing it, and if you are not in a situation where you can share visions and thoughts then maybe you are in the wrong place!

Whatever you do, please don't feel that the internet is the only tool for sharing; instead see it as a fabulous starting point. At Ernst and Young when I was there, consultants started to post issues that they were encountering for the first time up on the E & Y intranet. The volume of answers coming back from around the world was amazing. It was like posting letters to *The Times* and receiving instant replies from all their readers.

Look upon sharing your embryonic ideas as creating the bedrock of your future ideas team.

Share: Mind Step 1 Compose a circle of influence

Surround yourself with an emotionally supportive yet challenging crowd who will detonate your ideas. Input from others can really add a bit of sparkle. If you are lucky enough to be in an environment where you are able to really communicate and bounce ideas off colleagues, then get bouncing, but if not, take your idea home with you and use informal alliances.

'Holding on to your idea until you perfect it yourself often results in you finishing it too late. Share it, use drawing boards and watch the idea grow. It is not about validation; it's testing out ideas and assumptions that matters.'

Matt Marsh, Ideo

WORKOUT SEVENTEEN

◆ Create your circle of influence with 12 key players. What materials are you going to use to facilitate bouncing your idea around?

Share: Mind Step 2 Recharge your batteries

By sharing ideas you can gain the benefit and experience of different minds with different priorities, values and attitudes. No two pairs of eyes see an idea in the same way. Drawing on a wealth of mindpower will give your idea an extra power boost.

But too much work makes Jo a dull boy. Now is the time to party. For your own sake, the health of your contributors and for your actual ideas you need to make developing ideas a joy to be part of. So what can *you* do to create an explosive environment?

Well for starters …

◆ Use inspirational venues for your get-togethers, and avoid the office.

◆ Play games to stimulate ideas.

◆ Mix work and pleasure with combined events.

- Involve people's partners and kids.

- Use stimuli such as music.

This is just for starters – the real list is endless once you decide that playing is important, and believe me it is. Get those involved in developing your ideas to create their own playtime.

WORKOUT EIGHTEEN

- Research suitable venues for sharing your ideas; be as lateral as possible. Produce a shortlist of six possible venues.

What four things can you do to stimulate the group, e.g. what type of event, who to involve, what games to play?

Share: Mind Step 3 Take the flak

'A new idea is delicate. It can be killed by a sneer or a yawn; it can be stabbed to death by a quip and worried to death by a frown on the right man's brow.'
Charles (Hendrickson) Brower

There is of course a down side to sharing your precious brain-child. Criticism is inevitable.

Other people may not find your baby quite as attractive as you do.

Managing your emotions and being able to benefit from any criticism is a vital part of sharing. It means recognizing criticism for what it hopefully is, constructive feedback. Even if it takes the form of a daft ill-considered verbal attack, there will still be some way that you can use it and learn from it.

Only when you've established this can you begin to respond appropriately. Irrational, resentful and stubborn responses are not the way forward. Deciding whether particular criticism is right or wrong is an important skill. If it makes you think about your idea in a new light, then maybe you should use the criticism to either rebuild your idea or re-create a new one. Most importantly, Explosive Thinkers are persistent, they 'never say die'.

'Good ideas come when people with different perspectives work together on the same problem.'
Mary Ellen Hyde

The broader the church you embrace when you seek feedback, the more likely you are to solve a problem before it actually becomes one.

'Sharing ideas can be dangerous because this is when you're at your most vulnerable. You've got to choose the right person to share it with very carefully. A new idea is very easy to break.'
David Stuart, The Partners and D&AD

SHARE

◆ Use your sharers to detonate your idea.

◆ Compose your own magic circle.

◆ Share hard, play hard.

◆ No two pairs of eyes see the same picture.

◆ Others won't always find your baby quite as attractive as you do.

◆ Thrive on criticism.

◆ New ideas are easily broken – handle with care.

TRIGGER

Nobody is as clever as everybody; share wide, share early.

section three
constructing incendiary campaigns

hey you

momentum

No matter how good your idea, it will not explode unless you plan an incendiary campaign. The greatest success of Pokémon was not the original idea but the myth and the miracle of their communication and distribution plan.

This is where a virus

This is where your idea

YOU COULD SAY EXPLOSIVE

stops being a virus and becomes an explosive idea

stops being vunerable and starts becoming valuable

THINKING CREATES VIRAL ADD

'Constructing Incendiary Campaigns' will enabe you to build your brand and develop your language to score with the people who matter

chapter eleven
build

acquire your communications ology

The science of communication and how to construct ideas that mirror the way people think.

SIGNPOST

build

◆ Idea sorting

◆ Credo

◆ Parabolic thinking

◆ Create a new life

◆ The power of truth

◆ Prefabricate to replicate

Welcome to build

How many times has someone talked to you about an idea, or presented an idea to you, and at the end you haven't got a clue about what exactly they really mean? It's even worse if you instinctively feel that they have cottoned on to something good but you can't get a grip on why or what the next stages should be for anything to come of it.

Alternatively, how often have you been presented with a well-structured idea that made sense but lacked any inspiration or spark to get you going?

Build is about overcoming both of these problems, so you end up with a sound platform to present from, whatever method you choose to communicate your idea.

Build isn't just for big corporate types delivering formal multimedia presentations. The ideas here will work just as well in trying to persuade your partner to part with some of their hard-earned cash to fund some crazy idea you've got.

Build: Mind Step 1 Idea sorting

If you have any kids yourself or know people with kids, you will have experienced every type of toy from yo-yos to Gameboys. And if you have ever spent time playing with very young children you will probably have experienced shape sorters which, when I was a boy (back in the Dark Ages), were made of wood.

You have a series of shapes, round, square, star-shaped, triangular, etc., and a series of holes, again round, square, star-shaped and triangular. The object of this riveting little game is to put the right shape in the right hole. If you try to push a star into a triangle it won't go in.

Why am I telling this story? Well apart from giving me a chance to wallow in nostalgia thinking about my long-forgotten childhood, this game illustrates what so many people try and do day-in day-out – shove square pegs in round holes!

So the first thing to understand in building your message is, what shape are your audience's holes? Or in other words, how can you make sure that your message goes in?

Here are some things to think about.

One – it's a numbers game

How many things can you remember? Now be honest, if your partner sent you down to Tesco's with a random list of 20 things ringing in your ears as you closed the front door, how many would you come back with? In my case I would probably come back with completely different things like champagne, chocolates, car magazines, doughnuts and steamed treacle puddings with vanilla custard – blow the toilet rolls, milk and soap powder.

You may be the exception, but apparently most people can't remember more than seven things in their short-term memory without resorting to special memory techniques. The range in fact is five to nine, with few people above seven and quite a few, including myself, at the lower end.

So if you are trying to communicate your idea to someone with a long list of killer, drop-dead wonderful benefits, it is highly likely that by the time you are halfway through your list, many of the people you are talking to will have drifted off into a world of their own.

Stephen R. Covey sold over 10 million copies of his book, *The Seven Habits of Highly Effective People*. If he'd written *The Seventeen Habits of Highly Effective People* it would probably have bombed.

There are exceptions of course, like the ten commandments. If Moses had known this stuff we might have ended up with seven commandments that we could all remember, and who knows, adultery might have been OK.

Ideally if you want to make a specific point, limit yourself to as few illustrations as you can – three for preference, five is OK, seven is pushing it and nine is generally over the top.

There is also a view that odd numbers are more memorable than even numbers, so five and seven points are more likely to be remembered than four or six.

If you would like to know more about this, one book that explores it in detail is *The Pyramid Principle* by Barbara Minto (Financial Times/Prentice Hall, London, 1995).

Two – join up ideas

If complex ideas can only be communicated in small numbers, then you have to batch them together. In doing this there are four key things to remember:

◆ Start with one clearly stated point.

◆ Break that point down to a maximum of five sub-points that are summarized by the point above.

◆ Make sure all points in a specific group are linked together.

◆ Present all the points within a group in a logical order relative to each other.

Three – state the obvious

People are programmed subconsciously to group ideas together and create links between these groups as a standard part of memorizing. You need to explicitly state how you have linked your idea groups together and what logic you have used to do so, or your audience will jump to their own conclusions, which may not take them where you want them to be. What is obvious to you may be pea soup to them.

Four – if I've told you once

◆ Tell them what you are going to tell them.

◆ Tell them.

◆ Tell them what you have told them.

It doesn't matter whether it is a written report or a presentation, signposting and summarizing will help people absorb your message. Even in informal discussions, stopping the flow every now and then to check understanding and to make summaries will help.

Five – don't forget the detail

If you are writing your idea down, highlighting the structure is vital so make key lines stand out with headings, indents, underlines and bullet points, etc.

Use space and pauses to create emphasis. Use strong language – not swearing, I mean things like 'will' instead of 'might', 'but' instead of 'however', 'outstanding' instead of 'good'.

Avoid buzzwords like the plague. In particular, ban words from your vocabulary that are dry and empty like 'value creation', 'mega growth', 'quantum leap' and 'continuous improvement'.

WORKOUT NINETEEN

◆ It's time to practise idea sorting. Produce a list of everyone you know (minimum 100 to maximum 200).

◆ Using all the logic explained in Mind Step 1, create a presentation that turns your random list of 100-plus people into a logical story that anybody can understand.

◆ Present it to a friend and test your skill.

Build: Mind Step 2 Credo

As I said earlier, your idea credo will make or break your idea. It will bring your idea to life both for you and for those you wish to involve in developing it.

In my recent book *Brand Storm*, I introduced 'Wishbones' as a plain English blueprint for the success of a business, the elixir of life from which a whole business can grow. Your credo can do for your idea what a 'Wishbone' can do for a business.

So what are the key elements of an idea credo?

Vision

Describe the world in which your idea will live. Make it as vivid and as real as you can – if you can't make it live in words, why do you believe it will work in reality?

Dream

This is your personal dream for your idea. What are you trying to achieve? If you were dreaming up Pokémon, would you envisage millions of school children in every country in the world swapping anything they or their parents owned for your cards? Would you dream of mass hysteria and media interest turning what is basically a complicated playing card into an international phenomenon?

Are you dreaming big enough?

Purpose

- What is the underlying purpose of your idea?
- What makes you and your idea unique?
- What will your idea do?
- What are the most fundamental goals of your idea?
- What exactly are you selling? Convenience? Quality? Discount pricing? A dream? An escape?

Promise

- What are you promising to investors?
- What do you promise your customers?
- What do you promise your team?

Strategy

◆ What is going to make your card different from other collectors' cards?

◆ How will you deliver, market and support your idea?

◆ What will be the cornerstone of your success?

◆ What will define your success or failure?

◆ How do you intend to deliver your strategy?

◆ Who are your target customers? Develop a strong target customer profile to bring them to life so well that you can close your eyes and see them.

Virtues

When you really get to know someone you learn about their character, their personality and their virtues. What do you want the end users of your idea to learn about *you*?

Visuals and voice

◆ How are you going to present your idea visually?

◆ How do you want people to hear your message?

Once you have set out your credo, don't leave it there. Visually bring it to life and make it sing, keep it in a prominent place in front of you and your team.

WORKOUT TWENTY

◆ Construct a credo for your idea.

Build: Mind Step 3 Parabolic thinking

Instil some warmth in your audience with intensity, zeal and zest. All the things you put into generating ideas in the first place – purpose, inspiration and enthusiasm – must be transferred to your audience for maximum impact.

Take them on a journey, your ideas journey. Make it a story. Give them a bit of background information on where you got your idea from and inspire people with your idea's history.

Turn your idea into a parable and people will hear you. It has worked well for the Bible and trust me, it will work for you.

You may have audacious goals and visions, but if they are contained within sections headed 'Objectives' and 'Executive Summary' they will be instantly filed away in people's heads under 'just another one'.

WORKOUT TWENTY-ONE

◆ Turn your favourite idea into a five-minute play.

Find a victim to perform it to!

Build: Mind Step 4 Create a new life

'To pitch our launch idea to Nintendo for Pokémon we turned our whole office into a Pokémon forest complete with astro-turf, blue sky, waterfall and live rabbits!'
Mike Mathieson, Cake

If you want to wake up your idea, build it. Being able to hold, touch and feel your idea adds to its power enormously.

When I held the joyous position of handbag buyer for the retail chain Dorothy Perkins we used to call in samples to present at range reviews, but unfortunately we could not always guarantee what colour the sample would arrive in.

It didn't take me long to realize that if the sample wasn't in the colour that we wanted to buy, nobody would like it. The reason given was always some supposed aspect of design and never the sample colour. It became clear that even in a business where people were trained to view things subjectively, they couldn't see beyond what was in front of them.

Most people can see only what you put right in front of them.

Take the time to make your idea real and actual or it will wilt and die before your eyes.

'Bring ideas to life through design, mood boards, illustration, web design, models, 3D drawings, for example. Then execute them in house so that no idea is lost in the handover from creative concept to creative implementation.' Mike Mathieson, Cake

---

WORKOUT TWENTY-TWO

◆ Construct a physical mock-up of one of your ideas to bring it to life. Use any materials you like. Does it cut the mustard?

Build: Mind Step 5 The power of truth

Never underestimate the power of truth.

Simple honest points conveyed with integrity travel straight to the heart.

When the Tories used the 'Labour Isn't Working' strap line on their adverts, it worked because in one line they had captured the mood of the nation. However, when they used the adverts with red 'devil' eyes on Tony Blair, they wasted their money because it didn't strike true with the punters.

Be warned – don't tell lies, or even fibs for that matter.

◆ To test your ability to combine truth and tact, pick out a friend or colleague that you believe has a weakness or fault and articulate what action you think they should take.

Your task is to tell them in a positive manner. How are you going to do it?

Build: Mind Step 6 Prefabricate to replicate

'We use concise presentation techniques, visuals, soundtracks, live web-links, video clips, even actors and animals.'

Mike Mathieson, Cake

You must expect to use a broad range of methods to communicate your ideas. It may be actors, videos, flip-charts, opera, adverts, letters, e-mails, flash-mail, sandwich boards or even plain, old-fashioned talking.

To switch from one method to another seamlessly, deconstruct your learning points so they can be reconstructed simply on-site to fit a different medium.

BUILD

- What shape are your audience's holes?

- Never tell more than seven tales.

- Use joined-up thinking.

- Create your own credo.

- Talk in parables.

- Let the world actually touch your idea.

- Honesty works, honestly!

Trigger:

TRIGGER

When you tell a great story, your idea stops being vulnerable and starts being valuable.

chapter twelve
brand

own your own language

How to use your own language to maintain ownership of your idea as it spreads through your idea ecosystem.

SIGNPOST

brand

◆ A rose by any other name

◆ Own your own language

◆ Tools of the trade

◆ Attacking defence

◆ Value marks

Welcome to brand

'Inventions … cannot, in nature, be a subject of property.'

Thomas Jefferson

It is getting almost impossible to completely protect your ideas, and Thomas Jefferson's sentiment is rapidly being realized by the business community. The notion of ownership, particularly concerning business ideas, is changing constantly, and as your idea travels through your idea ecosystem you need to protect it against the idea demons.

Explosive branding revolves around establishing spiritual ownership in the eyes of your customer or target audience and is more about your own identity and psyche than it is about attracting and enticing customers with logos and tag lines.

Brand in this context is every component of your idea – you, the idea itself, all the people involved, any physical product or service you are hoping to create, all physical expressions of your idea, for example any logos, its voice, its reputation, its associations and endorsements, its customer perception and its total communication.

The earlier you start thinking about a brand for your idea the more explosive it will become.

Brand: Mind Step 1 A rose by any other name

It's all very well to claim you invented the next big thing, but it will get you nowhere fast unless you actually put a name to it. Choosing a name for your idea is pretty difficult. In fact, it can be incredibly frustrating to make a decision on the right name, one that encompasses all that you're trying to achieve.

At the moment there is a mad rush to find good names. The internet is the cornerstone of this rush as everybody needs a voice and a brand to sell it. The net has opened up bags of opportunities and almost a bag of court cases for each one.

In an ideas world your name is the gateway to rejection or acceptance by everybody – partners, potential partners, investors and customers. To Explosive Thinkers a memorable name is the first stake in the ground. It's like the Wild West land rush. So where should you start?

Morpheme mania

A morpheme is the smallest possible meaningful unit of a word. There are 600,000 morphemes, so in theory this means endless combinations. However, it does require a fair bit of effort. One of the best ways is to break your idea down into its core parts and then try and fit morphemes to these. Choose a morpheme for each part of your idea and see how well they fit together. But try and keep it short.

Universal language

Look for morphemes that mean the same thing internationally. For example, Sony is constructed around 'son', which means 'sound' all over the world.

Love and marriage

Finally, do your words fit together? Is there chemistry between them? Are they having good sex?

Fashion victims

Like everything, names are now a fashion item. For example, anything with an 'e' in front of it, like E-bay, etc., will be datable to within a couple of years and will shortly seem more old fashioned than leg-warmers and ra-ra skirts. Avoid this like the plague.

Think lateral

When you first start to think about a name, it is virtually impossible to think too broadly. If you are developing the right idea and you create the right brand, *whatever* name you choose will eventually stand for what you do.

Brand: Mind Step 2 Own your own language

The best way to brand your idea is to embed it within your own language and create a brand message that is the epitome of your idea. This will allow you to control the way your message is communicated and received. Essentially, choosing your own brand vocabulary means you are putting yourself in control.

Does it give out warmth? Go back to what you thought about for your idea's karma and use it to construct a brand language that communicates exactly the right aura.

Brand: Mind Step 3 Tools of the trade

Slogans

You may well choose to use slogans and thinking of these will help you when you're pitching. Slogans are all about understanding your and your competitors' positioning and setting yourself apart from it. It's also vital to consider the environment in which your slogan will live and to break the pattern.

Avoid self-congratulatory jargon. In fact, avoiding jargon totally is probably a good thing. Brands are no longer only about gimmicks – they've got to have integrity, and this should be reflected in your slogans and tag lines.

Websites

Once you have decided on a name, you need to register it fast. There is nothing more frustrating than coming up with a fab name and then not being able to use it! Branding on the net is big business and it's essential to get a good start. Your website is the reception area for your brand, where you and your customers come face to face and first impressions count. Concentrate on the needs and expectations of your visitors. Understand exactly how they want to interact with you. You can no longer rely on logos and tag lines alone. It's all about customer experience. At the moment a lot of internet sites are only mildly engaging rather than being entertaining or useful. Pre-empt the big shakeout by sorting out your site now.

Search me

Your use of words is key to making it easy for search engines and random surfers to find you, so concentrate on search optimization.

Get local

Whatever your idea, try becoming 'intra-local' to really connect with your customers. This is quite hard work, as it means customizing your offer to the individual needs of the smallest possible localities. Try street campaigning and street marketing or, to totally immerse your audience in your idea, embark on a local crusade.

Brand: Mind Step 4 Attacking defence

Destroying your competitors' core beliefs is one of the cornerstones of Explosive Thinking. When creating your brand this should be very much front of mind. Don't go down the 'me too' route, try the 'I'm a one-off' route. In other words, don't copy what they do, do your own thing.

Get a whiteboard and write up everything you know about your competitors' brand propositions. Try taking totally the opposite stance and see where it leads.

You can also try the same tack looking internationally. What is it that other countries take totally for granted and that you can challenge head on?

Brand: Mind Step 5 Value marks

Value marks are the trademarks of Ideapreneurs. Work hard to create value for your customers, when you're thinking about your idea and branding it – keep value for customers at the forefront of your mind. Consumer fatigue can only be combated with truth, dignity and humanity.

The transparency of the Human Economy that the internet has created literally means that you've got to say what you mean, and sell exactly what you can deliver.

There isn't room for false promises, so make sure you don't overestimate your strengths – consumers now have the power to hunt you out. Be your own brand custodian.

WORKOUT TWENTY-SEVEN

◆ Construct customer value propositions for your two new brands that capture exactly what is unique about your offering in terms of consumer benefits.

◆ List five ways in which your ideas will truly delight your customers. State how you propose to measure performance in these areas.

BRAND

◆ Choose a telling name.

◆ Own your own language and pick words with chemistry.

◆ Don't be a brand fashion victim.

◆ Think local, think global.

◆ Only brand what you can deliver.

◆ Be your own brand custodian.

◆ Create brand propositions that leave your competitors in disarray.

TRIGGER

Explosive branding is about fast spiritual connection, not just logos and tag lines

recognize

getting to and through the right people

Planning who you need in your idea ecosystem.

SIGNPOST

recognize

◆ Love match

◆ Powerful persuasion

◆ In-house roller-coaster

◆ Who's who?

◆ It takes all sorts

Welcome to recognize

'Ideas only happen fast and large when you manage your idea ecosystem.'
David Turner

With speed very much of the essence, planning who you need in your idea ecosystem is wickedly important.

My first job after university was in the buying department of the major UK fashion retailer Top Man, which considering I had no money and no clothes, was a dream-ticket job. The first thing that struck me, though, about retail buying was how complicated the whole thing was. You had more information than you could shake a stick at, covering colour, size, store performance, style category, old season, this season, new season, fabric, etc., etc.

If you took action on a Thursday it should show up in sales performance by the following Monday; everything could be almost instantaneous but nothing was simple. The ability to cock up what appeared to be dead simple was staggering, as I quickly found out.

One of the older, wiser guys took me under his wing and told me not to worry too much about analysing everything to death, but to study the info hard and fast, go with your gut feel and just do it.

But what you must do, he said, is know and be loved by the people that can save your bacon. Spend time with the warehouse managers, woo the area managers, visit the key stores and build up relationships with their managers. Be nice to the shipping manager and the point of sale controller.

And most important of all, don't wait till you have a problem – make contact when you have something to offer them, manage these relationships and they will look after you big time.

That was a long-winded sort of way of reinforcing what David Turner managed to say in a sentence and essentially it is what Recognize is all about. If you want to capitalize on your idea, recognize who you need in your world and develop a cunning plan to involve them. Do it while you have something to offer them rather than waiting till you desperately need their help.

Recognize: Mind **Step 1** Love match

Networking is now something else. It can't be cold and calculated any more. Although it may need a scientific approach in terms of organization and preparation, it's not actually a science, it's an art. You can't replace personal, human relationships with corporate veneer.

Work with those you love or at least those you like whenever you can, and if you don't like them to start with, try to find some common personal ground that you can use as a catalyst for some common thinking. However, always remember the old adage: 'Keep your friends close, but your enemies closer still.'

> **WORKOUT TWENTY-EIGHT**
>
> ◆ Make a list of the key people that the people you know, know.
>
>   In other words, write a list of all the important people known to your friends.
>
> ◆ Plan how to get to know these people and you've started to network.

Recognize: Mind **Step 2** Powerful persuasion

Have you ever been in a meeting when someone has completely trashed your project just because they're coming at it from the wrong angle? To get round this, you need to look behind your audience's facade and find out where they are coming from.

Examine your core message and ask:

◆ What can I offer this specific audience?

◆ What barriers might this individual or individuals put forward and why?

- How can I overcome these?

- What common ground (values, experience, goals) do I share with the audience?

- What do I want out of this person, or these people?

You can't persuade anyone unless you know them and know their priorities. Recognize is not only about finding the right person to tell your idea to, it's about making sure they understand it by understanding them. You need to develop antennae for understanding, not judging, your audience. Persuasion is all about connecting with people and the only way to do this is to understand each other.

Concoct your own network of inside sources to identify the motivations of your target. This will help you to pitch individually – you can't use the same pitch over and over again.

Recognize: Mind Step 3 In-house roller-coaster

If you are working within a company, who you talk to about your idea may well directly affect your career and what your colleagues think of you. If your idea goes down the pan, are you going to follow it?

Remember this, inside or outside a company the rules are the same – those you need, you need 100 per cent. There are goodies and baddies everywhere, some people will be a veritable goldmine and others will be out and out villains waiting to steal your idea.

There are strong advantages in keeping your idea within your company. You will be able to reap the benefits of existing infrastructure, taking away many of the headaches that classical entrepreneurs face, such as finding basic office equipment. There will also be a huge amount of experience to feed on and you're likely to get much more sympathy than if you were just dealing with investors. You also have the advantage of pitching your idea with the support of your company endorsement.

However, at least until recently, big companies have not been known for their ability to nurture grassroots ideas. If your company doesn't have a process for nurturing ideas, for example an in-house incubator, then capitalize on other young ventures that are successful and use this success to push forward your own idea.

Nevertheless, if you launch your idea within your company you're probably going to come out behind the Ideapreneur who launched through outside sources. You will make some money but it won't be the big time – risks are lower and the reward will be less.

WORKOUT TWENTY-NINE

◆ Produce six good reasons to promote your idea within an existing company.

◆ Produce six good reasons for looking at outside support.

◆ Compare the various pros and cons.

Recognize: Mind Step 4 Who's who?

So who can you talk to about your idea?

Your boss

Not a bad place to start. If you are working in a decent company, you should have a great relationship with your boss. If you haven' t, you are either in the wrong company or they are. Either way, try and engineer a change.

The boss's secretary

Developing good relationships with secretaries has often proved a wondrous source of insight for me. But remember they will have encountered every type of slimeball, from over-eager photocopier salesmen and over-sexed trainees to over-the-top managers, so try to be a bit different. Be real, be kind, involve and help them before you need them to help you.

The boss's bosses

Tricky on occasions but worth it. Approach with caution, but do it.

Colleagues

Bring them in early – you'll need them.

Other departments and potential partners

The same applies – you never know what you might learn and they can be great detonators for you.

Friends

Good friends can open up a whole new universe for you. These guys care about you and if they're really good friends, they may even stop you making an ass of yourself.

Your network

Your goldmine. How big is yours?

Customers and suppliers

Don't underestimate how much these people can help you. Get them on your side and nothing is too much trouble. You will be amazed at how helpful customers can be if they think you're doing everything you can for them.

WORKOUT THIRTY

◆ List four customers, four suppliers, four partners/company departments that you could talk to about your idea.

◆ How would you approach them and what would you say?

Recognize: Mind Step 5 It takes all sorts

If you're not currently working in a company or you just fancy riding off into the sunset, there are plenty of options out there in the big bad world. In fact, there's all kinds of funding available and it's getting better all the time with more and more companies deciding to invest. Companies as wide-ranging as advertising agencies, truck-makers, package couriers and independent film marketers are all trying to get in on the act. Companies have realized the threat of new up-starts and want to nurture them under their own wing. They themselves can actually take advantage of innovative technologies that could make or break the corporate parents' own futures.

Intel and Lucent Technologies have already poured millions into their own venture units. Everyone's got the bug. Artisan Entertainment, an entertainment producer and distributor in New York, helped market the low-budget but extremely successful *Blair Witch Project* on the internet. They have set up a $50 million venture capital fund called iArtisan to invest in start-ups. It's not just about getting their money back, it's about keeping ahead of the game and making sure you don't get eaten.

One of the best and most effective ways of deciding who you need to approach is to think about who you come into contact with every day and then think about their contacts and who they know. It might take several moves to get to the right person but it all counts. Group networking is an excellent route into the complex and often quite scary world of venture capital. Find out as much as possible about who the big guns are in your industry. Then make the call … who knows?

So what exactly are your options?

Venture capitalists are the big guys. If you're going to try this route then you need to be extremely confident of your idea capabilities and your own contacts. You also need to aim high – venture capital companies like to make large investments because they have money but not a lot of people. Venture capitalists seem to have acquired their own mythical status but they're not as mythical as angel investors.

Angels are wealthy individuals, but to brush against their heavenly wings, you'll need to move in the right circles or at least get your foot in the door.

Incubators deal on slightly different terms. They will help you progress your idea, from developing a business plan through finding funding to full development. What you ask them to do and the terms they will do it on can vary enormously.

Venture capitalists are now realizing that it pays to invest more than just hard cash. There are specialist venture capital shops which offer a full range of business development services like providing furnished office space, hiring recruiters and consultants in marketing and product development and fostering strategic alliances between new companies.

If you want to try something different, try Garage.com, who aim to fill the gap between venture capitalists and informal alliances such as friends and family. Their CEO is Guy Kawasaki, the software genius of Apple Computer fame, and his mission is to democratize the venture capital network. Venture capitalists tend only to deal within their own personal networks. In contrast, Garage.com are prepared to see anyone with a good idea and a good background. They look at every one of the 12,000 business plans they receive per year and then narrow them down to about 60. They also take a much smaller stake than most VCs.

WORKOUT THIRTY-ONE

◆ Visit *www.bvca.co.uk*, the website for the British Venture Capital Association. Founded in 1983, they represent virtually every major source of venture capital in the UK. The BVCA is dedicated to the promotion of the VC industry for the benefit of Ideapreneurs, VC practitioners and the economy as a whole. Since 1983 BVCA members have invested nearly £28 billion in up to 18,000 companies.

Find out all the information you would need to seek venture capital.

RECOGNIZE

◆ Build your network while you have something to offer.

◆ Never let corporate veneer replace personal contact.

◆ Choose your allies carefully.

◆ Work with those you like but keep your enemies close.

◆ Explore your in-house opportunities.

◆ Brave the outside world when you need to.

◆ Always recognize who's who.

TRIGGER

Ideas happen fast and large when you manage your own ecosystem.

chapter fourteen
score

seize your moment

A message for every situation, and how to make use of every opportunity to pitch your idea.

SIGNPOST

score

◆ Fast and furious

◆ Lift it up

◆ Corridor cuddles

◆ Phone power

◆ Don't forget your public

◆ International talking

◆ Well-oiled ideas

Welcome to score

Are you sharper than Alan Shearer, Teddy Sheringham and Emile Hesky at their best? Well you'll need to be if you want to become an Ideapreneur. Why do strikers cost football clubs so much money? Because they are the high-glamour players that shape the club's history.

Are you ready to make count every opportunity you get in front of goal?

Score: Mind Step 1 Fast and furious

Why hang around? As soon as you have had the germ of your idea, be ready to pitch. Your best pitching opportunities may well come before you are fully ready, but if you miss them they are gone forever.

Remember, Explosive Ideas hatch out of the egg ready to tell their story.

Score: Mind Step 2 Lift it up

I can't do it in a lift!

Oh yes you can! And it's more than likely that you'll have to at some point. It takes roughly 30 seconds to climb five floors so you've got to be ready and primed. Making the most of your time in the lift with the chairman has become a bit of a classic, but these opportunities do arise.

The elevator pitch is a bit pressurized, but as long as you're prepared you should think of it as a golden opportunity. Never get out of bed until you have your 30-second message at the ready. (It used to be a minute but lifts are getting faster.)

WORKOUT THIRTY-TWO

◆ Construct a 30-second elevator pitch using Explosive Thinking as your topic. Try it on a few friends.

Score: **Mind Step 3** Corridor cuddles

Bumping into someone in the corridor may not seem like the best first impression but it's a perfect opportunity to create or lighten up a relationship or bump your way through a hierarchy. Every contact an Ideapreneur makes is an opportunity in disguise – it's up to you to capitalize on them.

Score: **Mind Step 4** Phone power

Make sure you are a phone aficionado – it's quick, it can help build relationships and it keeps you close to your network. One of the biggest mistakes being made today is using e-mail when the phone is better. E-mail is fine for people you have a good relationship with, but for other people the possibility of pissing them off without knowing is endless because there is no immediate interaction. Think of using the phone before you use e-mail!

Ringing those you know is one thing, but what about those you don't?

Pros:

It is the next best thing to a face-to-face pitch. Even if you can't see them you can let them feel your passion.

Cons:

It's much easier for people to dismiss your cause over the phone than it is when you are in front of them.

As always, you need to know your audience. How much time will you get? How likely is it that you will be able to set up further meetings? Obviously it's not going to be possible to predict everything the other person will say but it's useful to think of possible outcomes before you make *that* call.

WORKOUT THIRTY-THREE

◆ Draw up a list of four friends who share your passion for ideas.

  Your task is to sell them *Hey You!* over the phone. Prepare an extraordinary pitch and start ringing!

  Let us know how you get on.
  lets.talk@team-murray.com

Score: Mind Step 5 Don't forget your public

There is a hungry public out there waiting for you, even if they don't know it yet. You've heard the old adage that no PR is bad PR? Well, it's not far wrong. Explosive Thinkers work out the right message and broadcast early. The more transparent the world gets, the earlier you need to be broadcasting your message, otherwise it may well get out anyway.

WORKOUT THIRTY-FOUR

◆ Create a PR brief for Explosive Thinking.

What are the four main selling points that will appeal to the public?

Score: Mind Step 6 International talking

Are you multilingual? Be ready to spread your word in 100 different languages.

This isn't just a language thing, it's cultural as well, for example:

◆ How well will your idea translate internationally?

◆ Can you afford not to pursue your overseas opportunities – might they come to you and bite you on the bum if you don't go after them first?

◆ Maybe your idea will just work better somewhere else, like in the States, for example, and then you can reverse it back into your own country later.

You can always seek partners to take some of the load off your shoulders so if your idea is genuinely explosive, what have you got to lose?

WORKOUT THIRTY-FIVE

◆ You have just been awarded the licence to promote Explosive Thinking in Australia and Japan.

Formulate a plan to promote Explosive Thinking in both these countries. Consider language, cultural and distribution issues.

Score: Mind Step 7 Well-oiled ideas

How easy is it for others to spread your idea? Winning someone over is one thing, but anyone you conquer with your idea has the potential to be a detonator for you. Whether it is via the web or e-mail or any other way you want, have you given your detonators the physical materials they need to make spreading your idea easy? Can people copy stuff from your website to forward to a friend? Do you tell people who they can pass your message on to? Do you encourage them to do so?

WORKOUT THIRTY-SIX

◆ Develop three separate ideas to make Explosive Thinking more slippery than ever.

E-mail us for feedback.
lets.talk@team-murray.com

SCORE

◆ Explosive Ideas hatch out ready to sell.

◆ If you can't do it in 30 seconds, you can't do it.

◆ Every contact is an opportunity.

◆ Become a phone aficionado.

◆ Broadcast your PR early.

◆ All Explosive Ideas have their own passport.

◆ Keep your ideas well oiled.

TRIGGER

Luck is what happens when opportunity meets an Explosive Idea.

chapter fourteen

section four
exploding on the scene

Ok, so you've 'Imagineered' and 'Constructed' your way to the right audience and the touch-paper of your idea is lit.

Now you need to

make sure it shoots off with a bang and doesn't just fizzle into the ground

It's time to build upon your Ideapreneur foundations, inspire your team and explode.

'Exploding on the scene' gives you that extra sparkle, the stuff that leaves your audience mesmerized, delighted and begging for more.

hey you

STAND WELL BACK...

momentum

perform

become a communications artist

How to perform your pitch with passion, tell
a story and sell your dream.

SIGNPOST

perform

◆ Strike a chord

◆ Art

◆ Locality and topicality

◆ Resonant simplicity

◆ Every second counts

◆ Look the part

◆ Be a magician, not a whiz kid

◆ Laugh? I nearly cried

◆ There's nowt so queer as folk

◆ Testimonial match

◆ Flatter to deliver

◆ Better by design

◆ Do it alfresco

◆ Play you charge card

Welcome to perform

Now is the time to literally stand up and be counted. Changes in mass media and TV in particular have changed expectations when it comes to listening to ideas. When I started working for BT, presentations were endlessly boring and endlessly long. Most of the presenters seemed asleep, which complemented their audiences perfectly, and going through the motions coupled with formality and intimidation were the order of the day. Not any more, business presentations must compete to communicate, messages must be sharp and outcomes well planned.

Less tell business, more show business.

All business must now be show business. If you want to move fast and bring others with you through Explosive Thinking, then high-impact presenting is a must.

Perform: Mind Step 1 Strike a chord

'You have to put yourself into the shoes your audience are wearing, ask what their hotspots are, not what yours are. What is their agenda, not your agenda?' John Cross, iSolon

Remember that when it comes to any presentation, be it from two to 20,000 people, the nearer you can get to audiences of one, the more they will individually buy your message.

You never present to a whole bunch of people, you only ever present to several individuals who just happen to be listening at the same time. Imagine you're having mini-conversations with each person individually. Don't make eye contact with the room – look one person in the eye for several seconds or one complete thought, then pick out someone else for the same treatment. If it is a massive audience, imagine people sitting at the back and pretend to talk to them even if you can't actually see them.

'Present your idea in a form that inspires and interests your audience, using examples that are specific to them. Ultimately, energize your audience by pitching in their terms and their personal benefits.'
David Stuart, The Partners and D&AD

Use their names, refer to conversations you've had with them. Endorse things that your audience have said at various times to tie them in emotionally to what you are saying.

I could go on, but at the end of the day there are endless things you can do and the best performers can do them all.

Keep your legs still, but move your arms to avoid looking shifty, show people the palms of your hands to look honest, lift your hands above your shoulders to embrace your audience, pause and stumble with your words to sound impromptu, the list goes on.

My advice is to buy a good book on presenting techniques and read it thoroughly but remember this – if you want to be a Master Ideapreneur you need to have read the book, got the tee-shirt *and* learnt how to create a unique style all of your own.

Knowing what to do is one thing, doing what you shouldn't do but with style is quite another – that is when you start to perform.

Perform: Mind Step 2 Art

Belle Linda Halpern is co-founder of the Ariel Group in Massachusetts and offers three-day workshops on presentations. Nothing odd in that but the difference is, she's a cabaret singer.

The moral is clear, don't present, *perform*.

Not before time art is forcing its way into business. My friend Miha Pogacnik is doing fabulous things. Recently he took the entire board of a major company into the heart of a full orchestra and used the music to change their views on business. Using the natural rhythms and symmetries of the music, he deconstructed the life and business cycles they were struggling with. Right on cue for an Ideapreneur.

Art transports people and you need to transport your audiences if you want to change the world with your ideas. Think painting, think sculpture, think music, think immersion and interaction. No idea need be too bold for Explosive Thinking.

WORKOUT THIRTY-SEVEN

◆ Develop a concept for bringing Explosive Thinking alive through introducing it to the arts. Use painting, sculpture, music or anything you like to produce a killer pitch.

Perform: Mind Step 3 Locality and topicality

A very simple way to win over an audience is to relate your pitch to topical or local issues that are particularly relevant to them like global warming, rail networks, etc. Just bring the real world into the room in a way that people can identify with. And you can't be too topical:

Read *The Times* and the *FT* on the morning before your presentation and I bet there will be a story you can refer to.

'Bringing realism into your pitch is absolutely essential. For instance, when T-Bone steaks were banned I began a presentation with "This is a presentation with the bone in it".'

John Cross, iSolon

WORKOUT THIRTY-EIGHT

◆ Read a couple of today's broadsheets. Identify three stories that you can link to Explosive Thinking. Capture these so you would be ready to use them in a presentation.

◆ Use them in conversation.

Perform: Mind Step 4 Resonant simplicity

Robert Kosberg is the 'king of pitch' in Hollywood and describes his job as 'telling bedtime stories to adults'.

Kosberg deals in the 'high-concept pitch', which is one so simple it can be reduced to a few key sentences or words. The film *Alien* was pitched as 'Jaws in space', for example. He also uses the 'TV guide' test – can your idea be melted down to two sentences that implore your audience to switch on and watch your show?

Perform: Mind Step 5 Every second counts

The second you lose someone during your pitch you can be 90 per cent certain you have lost them forever. The longer your pitch, therefore, the more chance that by the time you have finished, your audience will not be thinking about what you are saying but what they'd like to do to you.

'If you are given 20 minutes then do your pitch in 15 and give someone five minutes of their life back. *Never* run over time.'

John Cross, iSolon

For Ideapreneurs, finishing early is not an unfortunate dilemma but the result of practice making perfect.

The more you rehearse, the better chance you have of managing to time, especially when your flow is going to be disrupted by unpredictable questioning.

Perform: Mind Step 6 Look the part

It's a bit scary but in many cases half your initial impact may be based solely on how you look.

This can be taken to extremes, but it is essential to not only dress smartly but to dress right. Appearance is a highly individual issue – one person's designer chic, or garage cool, is another's Sunday boot-sale, so think long and hard about both how you want to look and what your audience like seeing.

'Besides pride, loyalty, discipline, heart and mind, confidence is the key to all the locks.'
Joe Paterno

The way you think about how you look will impact on your self-confidence. Not a lot of people know this (until now) but one sales guy I used to work with at BT said he always wore women's underwear under his suit for big pitches because he said it made him buzz more. Strange that he is now unemployed.

Perform: Mind Step 7
Be a magician, not a whiz kid

Technology, however whizzy, is now boring. It won't make your pitch, that's up to you and your personal magic, but it may break it.

The first base for any Ideapreneur is to be professional at all times. Be prepared to deal with it if, horror of horrors, your computer fails. Have a back-up plan, bring spare versions of everything, second hard drives, extension cords, spare bulbs, etc.

In the USA, people have actually created a business around saving people's presentations. They're called the Geek Squad, led by 12 'special agents' who provide 24-hour, on-site emergency response to computer problems.

Nevertheless, remember that you're not presenting your laptop, you're presenting your idea. Make sure you only use technology to display your message and not to replace your message. Your presentation can still be extremely boring, regardless of how funky your slides are. None of your technical know-how will matter unless you genuinely engage people.

Concoct visual enlightenment and illusion and believe it or not, people did get through presentations before PowerPoint and you can still do it again.

A good test of the strength of your pitch is to rehearse without slides or any back-up at all and see how you get on. If you can have them rocking in the aisles like that, then you are starting to rock yourself.

Perform: Mind Step 8 Laugh? I nearly cried

Did you hear the one about the two lesbians in the bath looking for a vegetarian eco-warrior? Only joking, but it shows that humour can often be a bit tricky.

Making people laugh and smile is the nectar of presentations but how you achieve it is less easy. Personally I prefer bizarre humour and a little irony to standard 'jokes', but whatever feels right to you, do it. Remember that you want your audience to laugh with you, not at you, and if they want to listen to a comedian they'll go to a club.

WORKOUT THIRTY-NINE

◆ Concoct a humorous story linked to Explosive Thinking.

◆ Concoct another humorous story linked to one of the ideas you developed in earlier workouts.

Perform: Mind Step 9
There's nowt so queer as folk

When I was a boy my Dad always used to say to me 'There's nowt so queer as folk', among other useful sayings like 'It won't get the baby a new bonnet' and 'Steady the buffs'. Dads are great, aren't they! But he had a point when it came to folk that is well worth remembering when you are presenting to them.

Within all these tactics don't forget basic manners and how to tailor these to specific audiences. For instance, be aware of international etiquette and make sure you research greetings and farewells if you're likely to come into contact with international business people.

For instance, Japanese culture regards any physical contact upon the first meeting as disrespectful.

Body language is also vital in terms of first impressions. Do you reflect the strength of your idea? For instance, to some, hands on hips indicates determination and the ability to take control, to others it indicates a stroppy sod.

Use gestures to add emphasis, but again be aware of cultural and national differences – one person's helpful finger is another's dire insult.

It may also be worth remembering that, as John Gray said, 'Men are from Mars, women are from Venus.' Consider that the people you are talking to won't always hear you the way you hear yourself.

WORKOUT FORTY

◆ List three things that you can use when addressing an audience that is largely the same sex as yourself.

◆ List three things that you would use when presenting to an audience of the opposite sex.

Perform: Mind Step 10 Testimonial match

People like to hear references to people they know, to people they would like to know and people they admire, but be careful. Be genuine – talk about people you have actually met, don't be a name-dropper and always try to maintain a vestige of humility.

The most successful people I know are either naturally humble or have mastered the art to perfection. I was working with Sir John Harvey-Jones a while back and the event involved an overnight stay at a hotel. In the middle of the night the fire alarm went off, and out we all trooped into the cold night air. Even at three in the morning, wearing dressing gown and slippers, Sir John was charm itself, asking pertinent questions of those around. That's the mark of a true gentleman and Ideapreneur.

Perform: Mind Step 11 Flatter to deliver

Don't overdo it, but it is important to make your audience feel special: 'I've come to you because of your immense experience in …' Furthermore, if they're the first people you speak to, let them know that you chose them first because you thought they were the most important.

Perform: Mind Step 12 Better by design

I've talked about it earlier but design shouldn't be an afterthought to your idea or to your pitch. If you close your eyes, can you see what a Volkswagen Beetle, a Mini and an E-Type Jag look like? The chances are you probably can!

Close your eyes again and try to see three modern cars, for example the Suzuki Ignis, the Proton Wira and the Peugeot 607. How did you do? It's not as easy when distinctive design isn't part of the original idea.

The same will apply to you and your idea. If you want to be memorable, design it in from the beginning, from the first germ of your idea through to your presentation support material and even the environment you want to present in.

Perform: Mind Step 13 Doing it alfresco

Try doing it outside, in a hotel, a restaurant, a museum and, without a doubt best of all, in a park on a sunny day. Explosive Thinkers are never confined by walls.

> **WORKOUT FORTY-ONE**
>
> ◆ Choose a fabulous location for presenting your idea that would make a massive impact. How would you manage the logistics of presenting there?

Perform: Mind Step 14 Play your charge card

Now for the really serious part – asking for money and explaining how your idea is going to make it. The key points are: be bold, be clear and don't be shy or apologetic. Would you lend money to someone who looks shifty?

If getting into your audience's shoes is generally important, then when it comes to money it is more important than ever. This is the time when you need to have seriously evangelized your case before your big day. And don't forget your detonators – this is where they come into their own.

'Always try and exceed expectation and put more effort into your figures than can be humanly expected. Take all the time you need to make your numbers shine.' David Stuart, The Partners and D&AD

WORKOUT FORTY-TWO

◆ Use a real project (if possible) that you have worked on recently and consider how you would pre-sell the financial implications to the relevant parties.

◆ Consider how to project your numbers in the best possible light. What figures and key ratios should you use? How much information should you provide? Do you want to present your figures at the start, middle or end of your presentation, or use a combination of all three?

PERFORM

- Put yourself in your audience's shoes.

- Present to an audience of one.

- Use your art to transport your audience.

- Make it local, keep it topical.

- Be quick and give your audience their life back.

- Be a magician, not a whiz kid.

- Flatter to deliver.

Trigger:

TRIGGER

All business is now show business, but money still talks.

chapter sixteen
provoke

be unforgettable

Create a personal myth, deliver high impact and make people think they're lucky to be in the presence of a legend and their million-dollar idea.

SIGNPOST

provoke

◆ Break dance

◆ Colour your emotions

◆ Americana

◆ Oration

◆ *Psycho* moments

Welcome to provoke

With Perform under your belt you should be feeling pretty confident about pitching your idea. We could put you on stage now – but we don't want to do that.

Performing is good but Master Ideapreneurs go further, they enter the realm of Provoke.

Do the unexpected and achieve the unbelievable

Close your eyes for a moment, relax and think of all the pitches you have seen during your life. Those you have seen on TV, in a theatre, or conference hall, the fully staged pitches and the impromptu ones. Pitches from politicians, leaders of industry, trade unionists, activists, work colleagues, friends and relatives.

How many have grabbed you by the throat and demanded your attention? Of those that have wowed you, what can you remember about the content and what can you remember about the person or the delivery?

The chances are that you cannot remember many specific pitches, and of those that you can remember, the person will be far clearer than what they said. Why is this the case? Simple – very few people know how to provoke and it is a real shame for everybody. Because most people don't make their ideas stick the world misses out on some great ideas.

To illustrate what I mean, watch some off-peak live coverage of the House of Commons when your average backbench MP is on their feet. What a load of rubbish. Here are the people who supposedly have our lives in their hands and can they string two proper sentences together? Can they hell.

They read from scrappy bits of paper, they shake, they look down at their shoes, their content is boring and, to add insult to injury, half of them look like they have just emerged from the bushes in Hyde Park, which based on the current state of play might be true.

If these MPs read *Hey You!* they could be dangerous.

But don't let's be complacent – without Explosive Thinking and Mind Play the same fate could await us all. So on with Provoke!

Provoke: Mind Step 1 Break dance

If you've read Perform and tried the workouts you will already be head and shoulders better than our MPs, but Provoke is about scaling even greater heights.

Now is the time to forget all the rules and do your own thing; it's 'break dancing', not the quick step.

We already understand the importance of destroying people's core beliefs and creating mental anarchy, now is the time to do it. Think about this in choosing your content as well as how you present it.

'Break dancing' is an attitude of mind as much as it is about skill.

Confidence is all. If you want to be extraordinary, believe you are and you will be.

WORKOUT FORTY-THREE

◆ Pick out one politician and one work colleague who are the best performers you have ever seen. List three things they do that you could build on.

◆ Look at the way you present today and choose three rules that you are going to break next time you pitch.

◆ Decide what three things you can do to leave your audience begging for more that you have never even thought about before. Think totally and utterly laterally on this, or all you will do is cover the same old well-trodden ground.

Provoke: Mind Step 2 Colour your emotions

Master Ideapreneurs are true chameleons in every sense of the word. Just as chameleons can change colour at will, so can Ideapreneurs. Think back to an earlier section, 'The Extraordinary World of the Ideapreneur', and you will recall the way Ideapreneurs think in colour, not only black and white.

Capitalize on this in preparing to provoke. When you plan your pitch, colour code each section to set the emotional tone for your delivery. Mix and match your colours to create a roller-coaster ride for your audience. The more consciously you do this, the more you stay in control of your pitch, rather than becoming led by events.

Let's review the Ideapreneur emotional colour guide

Black and scarlet are your anarchic side. Use these colours to drag your audience out of their comfort zone and when you want destroy their core beliefs, or even just wake them up.

Cream and limpid blue are for those moments of insight or reflection. Without lows there are no highs. Mixing and matching this and your black and scarlet side works well.

Purple and gold are for when you want to knock your audience out of their seats. These are the colours to use when outlining the benefits of your idea to the audience. Leave time for applause and pundits.

Green and rich orange are the colours of closing. You have already won their minds, now win their hearts. Make them like you personally and want to shake your hand. After having used all your other colours, green and rich orange are the ones to use to turn your audience into detonators.

◆ Think about colour coding your pitch. What four things can you
do to personify each emotional zone?

◆ Consider how to implement this in a way that will work for you
and make chameleon pitching a natural act.

Provoke: Mind Step 3 Americana

It pains me rather to say it, but when it comes to provocative
thinking, you have to take your hat off to the Americans. From Bible
bashers through politicians to business evangelists, these guys are
born provocative. They can even make water filters and food
supplements sound like they are to die for.

At BT we used a whole series of American business gurus to train
our sales and marketing teams. I remember one guy who was six
foot-plus, built like a tank and bald as a coot. When he exploded on
to the stage he would dress in black from head to toe, carry a silver-
topped cane and wear a black cape and top hat. He would then tear
about the stage like a ferret on heat.

Now don't get me wrong, I'm not suggesting you do the same, or
talk in an American accent, or wear your pants on the outside, or
anything like that. But I am suggesting that you provoke like these
Americans do. They have passion, energy and timing coupled with
supreme confidence. They also set their standards high and won't
settle for adequate when on stage.

Take a leaf out of their book but don't use the whole George W.

Provoke: Mind Step 4 Oration

To fully understand the power of the spoken word, listen to a speech by Winston Churchill or Martin Luther King. What they said was inspirational, the way they said it was explosive. Stop thinking of your voice as what happens when you open your mouth. Learn to master it as a professional singer or actor does and it will become a weapon in your Provoke arsenal.

Provoke: Mind Step 5 *Psycho* moments

To become a legend you've got to create an explosive atmosphere. As we have been saying, you can do this using the power of your delivery alone, but the icing on the cake is to create your own stage setting. Try using little extras like music, paintings or food, whatever's most suitable to your idea.

If you have ever watched *Psycho* by Alfred Hitchcock, as most people have, you won't have forgotten the shower scene. That was power, that was suspense. If you create the same type of atmosphere when you next present, you won't be forgotten easily either.

'Always dress the room, try to make the venue stimulating, avoid lengthy charts, keep it short, enthusiastic and to the point.'

Mike Mathieson, Cake

WORKOUT FORTY-SEVEN

◆ Using one of the ideas you developed in an earlier workout or Explosive Thinking itself, devise a stage setting that you could practically create.

◆ Put together all the things that we have talked about in Perform and Provoke and, using your best idea, develop an explosive, provoking, pitch that could make you the legend you deserve to be.

PROVOKE

- Break dance, don't quickstep.

- Believe in your own extraordinariness and you become extraordinary.

- Change colour like a chameleon.

- Convert your audience to detonators.

- Upstage like an American.

- Talk like Churchill.

- Put Hitchcock in the shade.

TRIGGER

Provoke your audience into believing that they are in the presence of a legend.

chapter seventeen
grow

bring your world with you

How to build a team culture around your idea
and inspire positive energy in others to
guarantee further success.

SIGNPOST

grow

◆ Passion play

◆ Trust you!

◆ Scared of commitment

◆ Partners for life

Welcome to grow

Grow is the third Mind Play section to focus on your relationships with the people around you. Grow recognizes that your idea is ready to fly but now needs help leaving the nest.

This is when your need for a strong team to crowd around your idea becomes clear. Even with clearance and financial backing, an idea needs friends.

Ideas don't become icons by living in an orphanage.

All the talk earlier about developing a credo for your idea will pay dividends now.

Grow: Mind Step 1 Passion play

'To inspire positive energy in a team, go out with them, take them out, talk to them, avoid the hierarchy, lose all internal walls, doors and windows – get together more!'   Mike Mathieson, Cake

I didn't get where I am today without passion and neither will your idea get far if those that surround it don't exude more passion than an Alpha Romeo, driving around Milan, full of hot-blooded young Italians.

What can you do to make people desperate to be part of your team? One key thing is to ensure that everyone has a stake in the game. As the pig said to the chicken as the smell of bacon and eggs wafted out of the farmhouse window, 'You're involved but I'm committed'.

Passion in a work sense rarely occurs accidentally, except at Christmas behind the photocopier. If you want a passionate team, be passionate yourself and make your passion so slippery that everyone else falls over on it.

If you want your team to love your idea, create a loving atmosphere.

WORKOUT FORTY-EIGHT

◆ What four things can you do to create a team that is as passionate about your idea as you are?

◆ What two things can you do to ensure that everyone who plays a part in the success of your idea is given a stake in the game?

◆ What three things will make your passion for your idea slippery?

Grow: Mind Step 2 Trust you!

Trust only flourishes if the person leading a team starts the ball rolling. This might not normally be an issue for you, you may be a really trusting person, but when we start to talk ideas things can change. No longer is this an idea, it's your baby and it's beautiful just as it is. And no one can love it more than you do, or look after it better because you are its Mum or Dad and so must know best. And then things start to go wrong. No one will ever trust you as team leader if you don't trust them to start with.

And just as with passion, you have to make your trust obvious. Up until this point there will only have been one vision and one dream, but now things will change. How are you planning to cope with gradually letting go of your vision so that others can contribute to it without losing your idea's uniqueness?

'If you want to instil trust in a team, start by giving them some space and trust them to do the right things well.'   John Cross, iSolon

And it's also worth deciding at this point what role you should personally play as your idea baby becomes an in-your-face teenager? Most people think that the natural role for them is CEO or MD, but this is sometimes far from wise. If you decide to bring in another CEO or MD you will need to trust them or your budding explosion may rapidly become a soft thud.

Grow: Mind Step 3 Scared of commitment

'Inclusivity is everything. Forget about the money for now – doing the right things for your customers and team won't cost as much as you think compared to the commitment it generates.'
John Cross, iSolon

Just as with trust, the commitment buck stops with you. If you want committed people and committed customers, commit to your idea first.

WORKOUT FORTY-NINE

◆ In what three ways can you show your team how committed you are to your idea?

◆ Think of two separate ways you can demonstrate your commitment to both your team and your customers.

Grow: Mind Step 4 Partners for life

However fast your idea explodes, and let's face it, the faster the better, remember that as an Ideapreneur you will be looking to repeat your successes. Your future success will be predicated on the partnerships and friendships you build up while working on this project, so neglect them at your peril.

GROW

◆ Encourage your team to crowd around your idea.

◆ Seek commitment, not merely involvement.

◆ Trust flourishes if you start the ball rolling.

◆ Give your team a stake in your idea.

◆ Decide what role to play in the life of your idea.

◆ Inclusivity is all.

◆ Partners are for life, not just for Christmas.

TRIGGER

Ideas never become icons by living in an orphanage.

hey you

momentum

chapter eighteen
aspire

prepare for greatness

How to use your ideas as your personal launch pad.

SIGNPOST

aspire

- How big is yours?

- There's only one cup

- Mucho credo

- H x 3

- Crusaders

Welcome to aspire

'I adore environments where I can build things from blocks that don't even exist yet'
David Stuart, The Partners and D&AD

Why are we here? Is it to launch one idea or is there something bigger, longer, wider out there waiting to be undertaken? I certainly think so and as we reach the last stage in *Hey You!*, that is what I intend to look at.

What do you really aspire to achieve with your life? Are you content to have passed your driving test or would you like to put Tony Blair and George W. Bush in the shade?

Aspire might help you find out.

Aspire: Mind Step 1 How big is yours?

Just how big is your ambition? Do you want to succeed just once, albeit big, or do you want to succeed time and time again? The mark of the true Ideapreneur is the desire and will to use each and every idea they have as the launch pad for their next idea.

This is what motivated people like Walt Disney and Branson to keep going, launching one idea after another. It isn't money it's the rush and thrill of the challenge.

WORKOUT FIFTY

◆ Where can your ideas take you? Starting with an idea you already have, map out four logical leaps that success with your first idea could lead to.

Aspire: Mind Step 2 There is only one cup

Each competition only ever has one winner. Everybody remembers world champions, prime ministers and FA Cup winners but no one remembers who the contenders were, or who was deputy prime minister or who the losing finalists were.

And so with the rest of life. Are you content to be good but not that good, or do you want to be the yardstick by which greatness is measured?

As a parent, would you want your kids to think of you as the best Mum or Dad in the world or is making the top 20 OK?

WORKOUT FIFTY-ONE

◆ What four things can you do to ensure that you dominate the world in which your idea is going to live?

◆ What two things would double the potential size of your ideas world?

Aspire: Mind Step 3 Mucho credo

You know how to produce a credo for an idea. Now is the time to produce a credo for your entire explosive campaign. This is a much bigger issue than doing it for a single idea. This is the manifesto under which you will unite all your partners and team players, not for a battle, but for a war. Examine your values – are they robust and attractive enough to lead an army?

Aspire: Mind Step 4 H x 3

So what do you need to step out of the mass of ordinary Ideapreneurs to the serried ranks of the Master Ideapreneur? If you adhere to the three Hs you won't go far wrong.

What are they?

Humility, hope and hunger.

Never lose your hope or hunger but stay humble, and immediately you will rise above the noise level. It is a strange irony that the ability to reach the greatest heights is founded on simple virtue. No, I'm not getting all lovey-dovey evangelical – it's based on simple fact. If you've really got what it takes, you don't annoy people by shoving your success under their noses, you don't easily get down or depressed, and you don't give up without a fight.

Aspire: Mind Step 5 Crusaders

When you succeed big time it may be time for you to reinvest in the society that gave you your success. Crusading is a central domain of the Master Ideapreneur. Just as Bob Geldof was able to launch Live Aid, the opportunities for you to use your success to good ends are infinite.

As with so many things to do with Ideapreneurs, this isn't pure altruism either. When you have created a platform to build from, crusading will expand your personal network faster than almost anything else. Doors will open that nothing else could even get you close to.

WORKOUT FIFTY-TWO

◆ Devise a crusade to spearhead your entire explosive world that links logically to your idea.

◆ Consider how it would grow your network.

ASPIRE

- Teach your ideas to leap.

- No one remembers runners-up.

- Let your credo lead an army.

- Feed the society that bore you.

- Build for a future that is just out of the reach of others.

- Use your ideas as your launch pad.

- Live in hope, stay hungry and remain humble.

TRIGGER

Strive to be the yardstick against which greatness is measured.

a big vote of thanks

Thank you for taking the time to read *Hey You!* I hope that you've enjoyed the book as much as I've enjoyed writing it. I have tried to make *Hey You!* fun as well as helpful – life is far too short and there are far too many fun things to do to waste time reading boring books, however laudable they are.

Tell your friends about *Hey You!* so we can start our own Idea Explosion and don't forget to e-mail me your thoughts as well, particularly when you are completing the 52 workouts.

Please also share your future experiences and successes with me. The most rewarding part of writing any book is the feedback.

Good luck with your ideas and I look forward to hearing from you soon.

Will Murray

lets.talk@team-murray.com

contributors

Stuart Armstrong, Cookson's
Cookson's is a worldwide on- and off-line tool supplier based in Stockport, Manchester.
www.cooksons.com

Sean Blair, Cofounder and Group Enterprise Director, Nowhere
Nowhere is a creative group of companies pioneering the future business of business, co-creating profound and inspiring innovation with a global network of clients, partners and associates.
www.limitednowhere.com

John Cross, Chief Executive, iSolon Ltd
iSolon identifies, locates and personally introduces experts and expertise to governments and businesses worldwide.
johncross@isolon.com

Richard James, Chairman, EB2B
EB2B is an IT company specializing in business intelligence products for the financial services markets.
richard@eb2b.co.uk

Matt Marsh, Ideo
Matt Marsh is an award-winning user-centred designer of products, services and interactive environments. He is currently Marketing Director for Ideo London. His experience includes both strategic and tactical work in the medical, consumer, computer and telecommunication sectors.
mmarsh@uk.ideo.com or visit *www.ideo.com*

Mike Mathieson, Cake
Cake is an ideas and actions agency which has four golden rules:
1. To be creative
2. To make money
3. To have some fun
4. That's it.
www.cakegroup.com

Richard Seymour, Seymour Powell

Richard Seymour and Dick Powell founded Seymour Powell in 1984. Since then, it has become one of Europe's most highly regarded product and transportation design consultancies. Their clients include Ford, Nokia, Casio, Tefal and Rowenta. *design@seymourpowell.co.uk*

David Stuart, Creative Partner, The Partners and D&AD

The Partners is a leading brand design consultancy and has been voted the UK's No. 1 creative agency for the past 14 years. David is also President of D&AD (British Design & Art Direction). *marketing@thepartners.co.uk*

Mike Weber, Community Development Consultant, the Ecademy

The Ecademy is an e-business education network providing a variety of face-to-face networking events and online news of training and resources for e-business professionals. Mike is also co-author of *E-business to the Power of Twelve: The Principles of Dot Competition.* *mikeweber@ecademy.com*

contributors

hey you

momentum